SLOW ARROW:
UNEARTHING
THE
FRAIL CHILDREN

D1603454

Slow Arrow: Unearthing the Frail Children

Essays from 9600 feet

Kathryn Winograd

Saddle Road Press

Slow Arrow: Unearthing the Frail Children
© 2020 Kathryn Winograd

Saddle Road Press
Hilo, Hawai'i
saddleroadpress.com

Book design by Don Mitchell
Cover photograph by Kathryn Winograd
Author photograph by Cassandra Vagher

ISBN 978-1-7329521-4-0

for my mother,
root spring and wandering star

my father,
trace fossil

for Leonard, my daughters,
granite and gossamer

CONTENTS

PREFACE

What's past is prologue
— Shakespeare, *The Tempest*

"Here," Leonard says and grinds his bike to a halt on Phantom Canyon's washboard road that leaves us bone-jarred. Elk and deer hunting season in Teller County and we have forgotten to wear orange. Gold King Camp signs—*Patrolled by horseback. Trespassers prosecuted*—hang from the barbed wire that separates us from private hunting lands and their deep wooded slopes. Hunters in camouflage, four to a truck cab, gun past. Wave.

A few months ago, off-season, we pedaled toward a man laughing by the open door of his pickup. A rifle with a full spotting scope lay on his front seat, while between his front bumper and the bullet-ridden water jugs and metal cans of his make-shift shooting range, a deer delicately picked its way across the road.

Leonard bends down, fishes something out of the dirt. An old bolt, blunt-nosed and corroded. Its flakes of iron stain my hand.

"A spike from the old railroad track," he says. "They're everywhere."

Then gunshot claps through the trees and ricochets down the road cut. And then again and again the hunters fire, our jackets frayed against the cold air, against the stray bullet we imagine, the deer with its small velvet of antlers we name dead.

I came to these 40 acres parceled out of an abandoned high meadow cattle ranch thinking it refuge from the worlds I had no control over, a sanctuary like the Ohio farm my mother and father bought almost unseen, climbing into it over a graveyard fence more than 40 years ago. Instead, I found this place to be the center of everything, found that one cannot migrate out of this world but must confront it and learn to decipher and accept the metaphors it gives.

Gold King, Moose, Anna Lee, Dead Shot, Anaconda— these are the names of the mines that pockmark these mountainsides we drive past with their rust and sulphurous spill of waste rock tailings. I say the words of the mine here— *assay* and *ribs*, *winze* and *whim*. And history walks through— the nameless Chinese laborers, who centuries ago cleared boulders for the three foot narrow-gauge rail road tracks of the Florence and Cripple Creek Railroad, and the mining men, who rode metal skips thousands of feet into the earth to single or double jack the *Mother Lode* with chisels and hammers and then plug the holes they made with dynamite. Or I imagine the perpetual darkness that blinded the burros bearing ore and fractured rock for these men through the mining tunnels, their horizontal drifts and adits, until, useless, the burros were left to wander the tunnels alone. Here they died. Burro. Sometimes, man. And now, myth walks in and I can't escape: Persephone eating the heart of the pomegranate or Orpheus of the golden lyre walking his Eurydice through the underworld.

"You can have it," says the woman who paints blue violets on antique Victorian glass in a sunny Victor shop. Victor once graveled its streets with gold. More than a hundred years ago, I could have walked the underground mines five miles to Cripple Creek and never once seen sky, never once risen above earth, a flesh and blood Persephone forever wandering the underworld. Except I would never have been allowed to enter the mines, despite the old mining vocabulary of "mother lodes" and "pregnant ores." Women were *bad luck*, sure to cause explosions or cave-ins if they entered the underground chambers of a mine, this superstition said to have risen out of the specter of grieving widows hovering at the mouths of mines, after the earth rocked beneath their feet. See how history and myth spill out everywhere? I hold out the chunk of gray rock the woman says her husband, a mine worker, picked up from the roadside for its stripe of purple. *Fluorite?* I wonder, which I read spurred the poorest miners to dig tunnels into the earth for its promise of gold.

"Here," she says, "between the purple and this thin line of quartz." She rubs her finger against the vein. "That's what they looked for."

She holds the rock to the window sun.

"See? The gold shines everywhere."

For more than a decade now Leonard and I have lived when we can on these outskirts of a mining district. The Cripple Creek and Victor signs that the county or the mining company or the state posts warn us the mines are active. Victor, "City of Mines," was once home to some 500 gold mines that held telluride gold, a rare gold infused with silver. Rotting head frames, "gallows frames," miners call them, rise above the vertical mining shafts, stipple Battle Mountain and the western horizon where the Sangre De Cristo mountains sprawl—named *Blood of Christ* at sunset, it is fabled, by a dying Spanish Padre seeking gold. Evenings, walking down the lane to this cabin built for us by timber framers and out of work craftsmen, the Sangres cresting our metal roof, I see the flared peaks with a dead man's eyes.

I try to record this niche and its gold, to be a good citizen of this tiny earth I am only guest to that seems to span whole worlds, where jets travel the crosswinds from the Four Corners and distant glittering valleys light the just-dark. When I set my sights on my fellow travelers that sometimes migrate a thousand miles to nest on our porch or feed from our sugar water, this wedge of land becomes its own telescope into the wider world. There is something of exhilaration in starting out with nothing more than a glimpse of a grainy iPhone image of a mysterious pronghorn on our land and then following an unknown trail that takes me through Rufous hummingbirds and high-powered rifle shooting ranges and the 7000-year-old bones of Indians buried alongside a highway to the politics of little publicized state and federal policies.

Caldera volcanoes, Late Eocene fossils, mines and coyotes, hummingbirds and droughts, old fires and husbands and fearful mothers—how do I begin to reshape these stories, to find the gallows ways of all their hidden mines? On windless mornings, I can hear, past Big Bull Mountain and the faint drone of open pit haul trucks, the hundred-year-old steam engine riding the narrow-gauge tracks of the Cripple Creek and Victor railroad, toting tourists past broken mines to new ones so immense they delay the sun's rise. This train is all that's left of the fifty-three a day that traveled here in the gold rush years up Phantom Canyon from Florence and Canon City or past Divide and Florissant and then hauled gold from the mines back down to the processing mills, more gold than from the gold rushes of Alaska and California combined.

The old miners dubbed what I think of as "half-starts," the single shaft mines that dot the high meadow ranching land surrounding Victor, "glory holes," which were dug too often in vain by the poorest of miners. The glory holes on these 40 acres are nothing more than chiseled bowls, slight depressions pick-axed out of the rotting granite just beneath the tenuous wildflowers and the roots of our aspen colonies. I know them by the chunks and cubes of granite and rose quartz that pile downhill from their mouths, the deepest glory hole a precarious ten feet that my dogs nose the precipice of, before I whistle them back from these testaments of hope and hopelessness.

My neighbor Tom has a forty-foot deep glory hole. A rotted wood ladder leads down to a darkness we so fear to enter now. He fenced and capped it with a bolted trap door, safeguard against the oblivious Angus cows grazing our leased lands or the unwanted hunter suddenly dropping into the nether world and forced to drink at the river Lethe. Even out of the abandoned refrigerators and the household detritus thrown down into some of these glory holes by long ago homesteaders and more recent rave-loving hippie contemporaries, the myths rise. These glory holes are more than a hundred years old. I think men saw the rainbow of purple fluorite and pink quartz and dreamed of veins of gold leading to the mother lode or to glorious "vugs," cavities in the rock that hung below the scree of this riddled land with their thumbnails of gold, gone now.

I understand myth to be about the biological: that just as a species of animals share instincts and behaviors and rituals, so do we. And that whatever our ancestors did, and thought, is still within us, tattered remnants that come to us in dreams we turn to myth.

"Would you want this to be your death bed?" Leonard asks me, pointing to the daybed I bought at a garage sale. We have been talking about my mother, who tells us she wants to die, who has chosen me, a daughter she has not lived with for over thirty-eight years, to steward her through oncoming blindness and death, even as this daughter tries to understand what it means to steward the land given to her for this little time on earth. My great grandmother's quilt, the one she cut and pieced together by hand, the one that hung years over my mother's farmhouse stairs, hangs above the daybed next to the small window we moved last minute in the cabin framing

15

so that it could swing out to the woods and the phantom spring below our cabin that beckons cow and coyote. Three needlework bird tapestries frame the back wall of reclaimed wood, stitched by my mother in honor of her mother with the little money her mother had to give at her death.

"Twenty-five dollars," my aunt tells me later, "all our mother had. Can you imagine?"

Above the Goodwill dresser, the quick deer study painted in oil by my mother's great grandfather, the picture Leonard always mutters over, teeters from a nail above the rose-colored vases I collected for our daughter Kitty's wedding.

I look at Leonard. He sits in the cushioned rocking chair I nursed our twin daughters in, where my mother used to sit when she visited the cabin. The stitching my mother did when she was young is so precise, so uniform: what she has always prided herself in. "A fine cheese," my sister and I always said, "sure to be sharper with age." Now our mother cries often, a mother I did not expect, sometimes pushing me away and I am brought back to my childhood, fraught with mute signals from a loving but demanding mother I trained myself to understand.

"It's why I never believe anybody's words," I used to tell the boyfriends who said they loved me. "It's what you do that matters."

In my study closet down in the suburbs is a tiny folded up piece of embroidery stitched by my grandmother, celebrating the day of my birth. It is made up of sagging loops of yarn and missed stitches. "My mother was clearly not herself when she stitched this," Mother says, generations, I recognize, repeating themselves. "Her work was always a perfectionist's." I remember visiting this grandmother, the tiny sparrow she had become fluttering before us, sparrow who did not know her own daughter, her own granddaughter, embodiment of my mother's fears.

Leonard waits for my answer, though after all these years together, he already knows it.

16

Am I ready for this? Are we, as Jung says, really part of a collective unconsciousness that goes beyond time and world and landscape and enmeshes us all, the randomness I thought surrounding us creating its own patterns, weaving its own little doors that I always tell my students their writing makes for them, for us to walk through into the human and wild heart?

Above Leonard hang the Victor hearth broom woven of broom corn by an antique broom winder and the wood I salvaged into a shelf for a vaseful of feathers—hawk, flicker, owl—and the small round nests we keep stumbling over in the woods. Outside the window, shadows of bluebirds, metaphors for the soul's rise, swoop past, the birds strewing the porch beams with wild grass they've borne from the ground to plaster into the nests we'll sit so carefully beneath late springs and early summers, long after my mother has left us, the small cries of nestlings punctuating the rhythmic return of these paired birds, cycle of rebirth in everything here: birds, grass, the green returning aspen promising us gold.

"Yes," I say.

BREVIARIES OF THE GHOST

*Art is an organ of human life, transmitting
man's reasonable perception into feeling.*
                                        —Tolstoy

THIS WAS SUPPOSED TO BE ABOUT the dying Western aspen
and the long litany of their probable ailments: drought,
SAD, leaf rollers, heart rot. And I was going to stand here,
the whole time, with a bundle of cut saplings in my forlorn
arms in this little forty-acre mountain microcosm alongside
Phantom Canyon, a winding road where once the Florence
and Cripple Creek Railroad carried gold the color of frost out
of Victor and Cripple Creek mines.

Dog hair—what I am holding. I looked it up. The Forest
Service term for the multitudinous sucker shoots that an
imperiled aspen colony throws out from its roots and, get this,
its "teats" beneath the soil. These sickly half-start saplings I'm
holding are the desperate attempts of my little dying forest
to re-clone itself—representatives of what is said to be the
sudden die off, Sudden Aspen Decline, (SAD), of over one
fifth of Colorado's aspen trees since our drought of the early
2000s.

That was what this essay was 'supposed to' be about.
And then there are my children's shoes hanging from our
suburban garage rack, four thousand three hundred and
twenty-three feet below Phantom Canyon in a place called
Columbine Knolls, one mile from the high school where two
boys in trench coats slaughtered the children I read about on
the stone markers of Rebel Hill, their parents still bumping
against me in the local grocery store. Kitty and Mira have
long since graduated from Columbine and college yet still

their childhood shoes bang my hip every time I squeeze past them and the car to dump the kitchen garbage.

Can you see the open garage? Moon in the elms for lyrical effect? Its whiteness we all know to be rock that I'll call *limpid, barely a veil*? Now the daughters trot out, twins soon to be five, and I line them up—curled hair, matching sweaters, pink-laced roller skates—alongside the elementary school's chain link fence where I once cried on their first day of kindergarten and then again first grade—their time with us, do you see it, gone faster than the whole circling of the moon?

But that's not the story. I think. Not even the fact that just four weeks ago, I hired a young guy named Joseph from Kansas with an elastic hair band wrapped around his goatee and a chainsaw parked on his shoulder. He felled nineteen of my standing dead, my "ghost" aspens, and numbered each rotted stump with orange spray paint so I could pay him twenty-five bucks per tree. By that time, I did not lose even a single tear.

Some 26,000 years ago, or 25,920 years to be exact, plus another 14 or so since the start of the millennium, we had no north star above the wobbling earth, no Polaris to point to along the earth's axis to steady us, to navigate us across seas, past dragons hidden at the edge of ancestral maps. "Axial Precession," the scientists call it, how the gravity of the sun and the moon, even Jupiter, pull the earth until, bulging at the equator, it shifts. The lesser stars, the blurred ones that the Neanderthals and the Cro Magnons could only see the milk of out of the corners of their eyes, give way bit by bit to the hard stars, the bright ones we eye now as true north. But even these stars will blur, wander off kilter until only absence is true. This is the story, I think—

Can you tell me, the dead son's mother asked me, *if his poems are good?*

Scientists ask if time is always linear, always moving forward, everything, scientists suspect, causality. In their *helical model of time*, time moves in circles around what they call an "emergent linear time axis"—only, sometimes, pushing off in a new direction, time both forwards and backwards.

The dead son's mother had signed up to take my writing class at the community college so that I could judge, she told me, the poems of her son. Handwritten.

My son died. He wrote poems. He was going to take your class. Can you tell me, she asked me, *are they good?*

For forty-five minutes, she wept in my office telling me the story of her son, a junkie, though she did not say that harsh word and I feel guilty saying it now, the son dead some two years ago in his thirties of an overdose.

Well, murdered, she said. *I would call it that.*

Tolstoy said, "It is not the artist who by his knowledge or skill produces the beautiful, but the idea of beauty in him itself produces." I remember my daughters, young, before their leaving, and myself, I see it so clearly now, as if barely out of girlhood, walking out after dinner—our yearly visit to my parents' midwestern farm. Evening spooled from the tree shadows, the sun a gold needle—do you see how memory wills itself into the beautiful?—at the spillway of my father's pond. Behind us, with our each step, the kitchen lights brightened, voices of my mother and father or the clean-up rattle of washed silverware laid out on stainless steel counters punctuating the gathering hush, an insistent farewell to *moment instant now* before the pines swallowed us. *There, here—*

All the time the dead son's mother wept, I listened and willed myself to sit still, though I'm ashamed to say, teacher that I am, I kept thinking the whole time how she got her story wrong, the old chronological "then and then this" narrative—that arrow of linear time that the helical scientists tell us does not exist.

"No way," I told my colleagues later, "is a grieving mother going to take my class for credit."

When does perception turn into feeling? I ask myself now. The morning my neighbor Tom cut down six trees for me—the most noticeably dead—I wanted him to cut down more, but as Tom said, the chainsaw was "out of gas and tired." I remember the first tree he cut down, undercutting it so he could fell it true and it would not fall back over the stump, "kick back" at him, and how it struck me on the way down instead, the sting of its branches on my cheek still. The cutting done, I walked through the dry fields with their yellow hefts of grass, spring's green elusive, and everything else, the trees, slowly dying. I have been trying to follow the ways of the Buddhists, as I understand them, to let go of all earthly possessions and care, for they are transient. Yet I have been known to cry at the cutting of a tree, the waste of it. I come from a wet midwestern country, a highway of exploding ditch grass, of cornfields edged by the constant gloaming of woods and the damp leaf litter of cyclical cicadas, not these aspen shoots ascending, descending, "weeds," another neighbor tells me, amidst the hard fixtures, *permanent* I want to say, that I keep naming into being for myself: this glacial granite I walk on, this scythe of the moon, these hard western stars.

Only her images stood out, circled us, the way my own lesser ones keep circling here: her dead son pounding at her front door, his broken car parked on her driveway where he slept and ate, and the train whistle, creeping through every scene, that she and her son listened for the same night whistle I hear along the far river tracks, tangled up with the wild cry of coyotes migrating our suburban water ditches or with the small pond of a father—just thought now, memory—bulldozed in as a refuge for the red winged blackbirds gilding the water still.

If we ask our daughters, our sons, will they remember time as we do? Know the feel of themselves beneath the stars, beneath the vast altitudinal sky with its long cycles of drought and heart rot, when they were such a part of us, pure palpitations of love at our pulse points: wrist, throat, thigh, ankle? Will they know the world as we do, *then, now,* a solitariness that embraces us for its single fleeting moment, and then again, and then, sometimes, if we are lucky, again, the way I am embraced by this moment, writing these words, melding past into present into utterance?

The woman kept coming back to it, the train whistle, the way I keep coming back to stars and trees and grown daughters or the mothers of dead sons, neither she nor I knowing what to do with these images, but knowing they have some kind of under life for us to hold onto, some causality beyond time and its helical axis. I read that a neurosurgeon named Susan Hockfield called the process of writing worse than "the squaring of a sphere." Is this why we write this stolid world, perhaps childless now, transient or permanent, as if we, I'll use this allusion, like the souls of John Donne's A *Valediction Forbidding Mourning,* could some "gold to aery thinness beat"? Is it beauty then, or the idea of beauty now? The rain in drought we pray for? The train whistle in the dark? Or the bull frogs that boom in chorus from a father's pond, a wheezy thrumming, half-heartbeat, half-exhalation I'll hear again tonight, this woman, who is now part of me, and my grown daughters and even the dead son stepping again and again with me into the gold rushes, determined to see the bull frogs' bulging throats, to touch *now* and *now* the thin mucous of their skin?

I live amidst dying trees. In the suburbs, my yellow maple died back branch-by-branch, withered leaf by withered leaf until I had it cut down. Now the leaves of the sunset maple by the south side of the house shrink, turn dun yellow. I inject the earth around its roots with liquid iron in hopes to stain its leaf veins green again, resuscitate what I know to be hopeless. Every week, for the past ten years traveling to this cabin, I have turned past Deckers, driven West Creek along the Hayman Burn, site of one of Colorado's most devastating wild fires, human-caused by a ranger who claimed she was burning letters of love in a circle of stone, whole draws of charred Ponderosa pine and Douglas Fir laying themselves down.

He wrote poetry; he was going to take your class; can you tell me, are his poems good? the dead son's mother keeps asking me. Why will I not answer her?

I remember one cool evening of stars, my little griefs as I see them now—our daughters away and their father poised at his telescope beneath the drifting galaxies—this image again—while our visiting friends sipped on wine. Then the quiet after their exit—how our shadows deepened as the solid moon deepened, no longer a veil, and far off, so very far off, how the first elk with quickening desire sang out thinly but sang out.

I want to tell her the story of the *gvrini*, a dirge sung by men who once scythed fields of hay to honor the dead beneath them, to score our thin mantle of earth as if some equilibrium, some rightness between two worlds could return. *Les pleureuses par la voix,* they call the song of scything passed onto these men, not by the women at the funerals who "mourn by calling" the listening dead, but by the women possessed, speaking with the tongue of the dead, the dead for the moment of the song finding their "temporary abode," some permanence, I think, in the transience, this mother already her son's oracle in this shifting landscape of grief, her son sung whole in the lexicon.

"Here," the caretaker said, this another story, a religious man meditating amidst the ghost snags of Shadowcliff, the Grand

26

Lake retreat for the summer workshop where I once taught. All morning I had watched him slowly clear away the branches of the dead trees he mourned. "Ghost trees," someone wrongly named the Lodgepole pines in the midst of this pine beetle infestation that has left 4 million acres of the standing dead. The caretaker marked each afflicted Lodgepole with orange tape until he cut into it, made the first notch cut to fell it true as Tom did. He wrapped each one in plastic, so that its swarm of brooding beetles, with their blue stain fungus that stops the tree resin from kicking the beetles out as they lay their eggs beneath the tree's bark, could not fly out, swarm to the next tree to begin their boring.

"Look," he said to me, and held my fingers against their blue exacting tunnels, his story, until I felt them.

He was here, you know, the dead son's mother said to me one evening as she stood next to me in the campus art gallery where both she and her son had once worked, turning the lights on and off, checking the security gate, snapping its lock on when the last visitor had left. We were listening to a young man read his poems surrounded by the artists' renderings of isolated worlds—what keeps slipping past us—and she said, *right here, a night like this, two years ago, he was here*, she said. *Here*. And I remembered Tom once pointing to the worn stump of a pine—*do you see the fire*, he asked me, and how I could see the grass, and the curve and swell of the underlying granite that held us, and then the charcoal mark from when the tree burned, but I could not see the fire.

In the language of tree cutting, the "felling cut" or "backcut," what will finally bring the tree down, must never be continued to a point at which no holding wood remains, no story of the living tree. I go out and search the aspens left for black spots of fungus or mold or the small worms that wrap leaves around themselves like tents, shrink the footprint of the colony, let light, horizon, air in.

And you were here, the dead son's mother says to me, *right here, a night like this,* and I am remembering a voice now, no face I can remember, her son saying to me, *my mother will be here, here,* and I can almost feel his touch, time in circles, the air above the vanished aspens cool and heavy with what the scientists call *virga,* those small breviaries of rain that never hit ground.

I sit at this cabin table now, while this mother I knew for only a time listens for the whistle of a train threading through the dark, the saplings I held in my arms long flung down. A house wren carries one frail piece of grass after another past the kitchen window while the late summer hummingbirds pulse at the sugar feeder I have hung from the pine, the one small sweetness I can give.

CANYONS

I SO SELDOM SAW DEAD BIRDS. Once I could count on that proverbial hand the times I had seen the bones of a bird: in Iowa, where I studied poetry, a sparrow thorn-pierced in a bush and a mile from the lip of this canyon someone named *Phantom*, hawk bones that whitened for two summers until I thought them airy as angel wings. And then the perfect bird I found near Annie's cabin, its whole skeletal skiff riding the long grass as if tethered by wind, until I placed it on my desk in a sepulcher of butter dish and tissue and the dogs ate it.

But, now, I stumble over the dead. In these fields, I have twice found owl and once hawk this past year alone, our dogs rolling in the slight remains and drifting feathers before I collared them. And through this very summer, I have found too many times a scattering of small birds at the base of our cabin, birds that have flown so blindly into our windows that they leave their tiny imprints smudged on the glass like faint breath or risen soul I could almost touch.

Perhaps I simply look for this quiet passing, something symbolic for that living tissue, that transformation my mother hopes she will enter soon between breath and stillness—transparent and so porous. The other day she says to me, "I can feel it coming; I am so tired now in my whole body," and smiles at me in a way I can hardly bear. Thirty years ago, when my mother was my age, she typed out her own book—what I had forgotten—a family genealogy she filled with stories about relatives my siblings and I had barely or never met, so we could remember what she did of her life, of her girlhood, her family, of our father and his family. She wrote this of her childhood years spent on a six-acre farm with her mother and father :

Jean was six years old when they moved to White Oak, and she loved this place. These were the golden years of her life. She was young, she was secure, she was loved.

Seven years later, her father, his heart weakened by childhood rheumatic fever, died at forty-two.

My mother often tells me, to console herself, of the young mother dying of cancer, the daughter of her friend who said later, "No one should ever lose a child," whose family finally took her from the hospital to a lake she loved where she died beneath a tree in the arms of her family. So much better, we both agreed—though I don't remind my mother of my father's death in a strange hospice, of how much better it would have been to be with him when he died not in a callow room of florescent light and linoleum floors but on the screen porch my mother had built on the back of their farmhouse, overlooking the pond where the bull frogs my father loved called from the water, the fish he named rising to the surface as if to catch breath. She knows that.

Perhaps I find fallen birds now because of synchronicity, everything in this world, as Jung told us, indeed tied together in that collective unconsciousness, our consolation of meaning, then, rising out of randomness. This fall, I will teach mythology at the community college: the world, and every god I think I know, turned metaphor for the uncontainable, for the essence of self, the mysteriousness that binds body to body.

Or a daughter to a mother.

She died a long cruel death, my mother wrote of her mother in her genealogy, *and it seemed unfair that it should happen to someone like Helen who had lived such a hard life.*

32

I think of this body of mine, how it taps on the keys of this laptop to write of dead birds and of a mother who waits to die and of the history of a canyon I hardly know yet. *In the cave of our mothers*, I once wrote, *the hands of their children are leafless trees.* We are still bound, even beyond a mother, to some primitive body, dust now, entering a cave, pressing its hands against the walls, and spewing ash or ochre into being, into the temporal, into the *other*—the burning fat of bison that I keep seeing illuminating the deep recesses, the swollen rock suggesting flank and elbow, and the glittering almost light of us.

> *When Jean was old enough to drive,* my mother wrote, *Helen would let her drive to Thompson Rd. Where she'd hike the woods and sit under a tree soaking up the stillness. Then she'd take a deep breath.*

When my mother sold our family farm in Ohio, I wanted only two things: a slab of creek rock and the steer horns capped by a bird nest that my father allowed to grace our barn all the way through my adolescence to the time I was a young mother of twins, living with Leonard some 1300 miles away in Colorado.

The creek rock I hauled home in a car after my final visit to the farm, the fields I traipsed through that my father once bush-hogged weekly tangled with thistles and stinging nettles. I remember it was a hot and humid summer, of too many foreseeable endings, my father's Alzheimer's making the farm's selling a necessity, my mother unable to stay alone with him behind the tumbled headstones of the Murdoch county cemetery where, unknown to us, we would soon lay him.

All that day, before I wedged the rock out of the blue creek clay I had sculpted as a girl into half-formed angels and blind effigies to give as gifts to my mother and grandmother, I walked beneath the black oaks and the transient Russian olive I still love, thorny and sweet with their yellow stars, past that spring-fed pond where we once skinny-dipped, my father's frogs that I had forgotten bellowing through a fecund air I knew I would not breathe again.

For many years after that, the creek rock with its ancient sea fossils leaned against our family room fireplace in the suburbs until Leonard and I built this stone cabin near Phantom Canyon and I begged the mason to mortar my rock by the front door, as if it were a mezuzah of a father I might still touch. Then, as my father spiraled into the dementia that inexplicably vanished him, (*Why did he die so soon?* my sister and I would ask each other for so many years), my mother un-nailed the plaque of horns my father had put there from the barn and shipped it to me.

"I don't want anyone to have to worry about me," she said just before she moved to her first senior community in Ohio and the horns arrived at my Littleton house via Federal Express. The bird nest was attached to the horns by means of bubble paper and masking tape entwined, as my mother described her, by an astonished mail woman. I nailed the horns and nest to our shed, memento of my father's farm, harbinger, I thought, of what is good, where it stayed until the winds off the Continental Divide funneled up from the bottom spring with a ferocity no midwestern bird could anticipate, and sheared the cap of bird nest right off and earthed it.

But I saved the nest, what I have always done with what others have thought bereft and cast off—a tattered snakeskin, a yellowed muskrat tooth, a chrysalis dangling from a wisp of grass I found by my father's pond and brought here some thirty years ago.

"Okay, Kath," Mother said over the phone, thirty-eight years after I had left home, fifteen years after my father's death widowed her. "I'm coming."

Jung said, "As far as we can discern, the sole purpose of human existence is to kindle a light of meaning in the darkness of mere being." I can say that less than a mile from the lip of Phantom Canyon, I live in a world of trace fossils: of ghost grizzlies said to maul a woman's arm, of Indian princesses said to bewail a lost betrothed, or of the dust of Chinese laborers blasted from a railroad bed built to haul gold, dust of body or gold blowing against me each time I ride my bike up Phantom Canyon.

And I can say that nothing warns you of the fall into any canyon. Here, a thin ribbon of water called *Eightmile Creek* trickles barely noticed out of a rancher's holding pond that Leonard and I bike past weekly. This water slips beneath us through a corrugated pipe someone built the lane over, then vanishes into a valley where our young daughters once circled grazing horses like wandering stars and then to the deepest of canyons. Eightmile creek carved this four-thousand-foot-deep box canyon, a narrow cajón cut by snow melt and underground springs into four hundred-million-year-old sandstone and the granite I thought so steady beneath my feet until my mother moved here, nothing, it seems now, to take lightly. Let the canyon flame and fire will thunder upslope, burn the uncertain hotshot and the smokejumper in firestorms and blow-ups. Let the heavens pour and a torrent of rain or snowmelt will crush railroads and flood inescapable canyons, whole worlds destroyed for new creations, for new worlds.

Let a grieving mother come to you and worlds open, close, open.

Katabasis comes from the Greek words for "down" and "go" and describes the act of descent—in mythology, the descent into the underworld, and here, the descent into a canyon haunted by one more phantom: my aging mother, who I have known from a distance all these years since I left home, a woman fearful of the macular degeneration and the glaucoma her doctors needle her eyes to slow and of the death she says she wants, my mother journeying here to be with me so that I might guide her to what I myself don't understand.

Over twenty years ago, while my mother listened to the eye specialist who said she would go blind eventually, like her uncles and grandmother did—"Why was her house always dark at night?" Mother said she always wondered of her grandmother—my father, a retired doctor, not yet diagnosed with the brain's degeneration that curled his own mother into a nursing home bed, sat in a chair by my mother and trimmed his fingernails, unspeaking, my father's Alzheimer's forever tangled up with my mother's diagnosis of blindness, my mother this blind seer I so gently tether here.

So they have had the good life, my mother wrote in her family genealogy of her and my father, (my father my age then, six years before he was officially diagnosed with Alzheimer's, though my mother labeled his sock and underwear drawers long before this.)

On the last page of that untitled family genealogy that my mother wrote, typed, copied, then clipped into three yellow school-girl folders to mail to my siblings and me, she carefully drew out our family trees. She added notes about a silver baby cup that belonged to a grandfather's brother and about a sampler stitched in 1843 by a fourteen- year old ancestor named Elizabeth Bradbeer (*on your dad's side,* she wrote), a sampler she carried with her from house to senior center to Colorado, where she finally gave it to me to hang on my living room wall. "There's no room for it here," she said when I helped her move into the tiny yellow apartment of this last assisted living home with its acre of gardens she could walk through.

But just before the family trees, just before she signed the book with her whole maiden and married name thirty years ago at the age I am now, this woman who sometimes weeps to die, wrote in the third person these words, words I can't forget, about the farm she and my father lived on for twenty-five years:

> *Kids, dogs, cats, horse, ponies, cattle, sheep, goats, rabbits. An old house that needed constant repair and paint, water pumps that broke down all at the wrong times, electricity that went out at the first crack of lightning, barn and shed roofs that leaked, grass that always needed mowing, equipment that always broke down during haying season. They loved every minute of it. Jean especially loved it. The first morning she saw the kids off in the big yellow school bus, she danced all the way back the lane for the sheer joy of living...*
>
> Jean Kamp Burt 1988

Once someone asked me to write why I live above Phantom Canyon, with "no wasted words" and in "any form." How I struggled to write that, knowing that even though chance might lead me to the readers' no-man's-land of the non-narrative, it might surely, too, lead me to the poetic sublime, that buried cavern of glittering light.

Why I have come here, in any form, with [three random] words, I finally wrote as my title, my first word, *forged*, wresting together those phantoms of a canyon I keep returning to: grizzly bear and princess and those railroad and mining workers who perished for the promise of gold. And then the word, *sawtooth*, what I wagered as reason two, as in *sawtooth of snow*, what each winter I walk now since my mother's arrival, teetering over new wing drifts and heart tracks.

And now word three, what I find today—my narrative for the reader, as I feared, pitched to the treacherous hereto of the non-linear—because, once more, I have stumbled upon hawk or owl, I do not know which, dead-still on a bier of

37

feathers and I thought *angel fallen* or *Icarus stunned*, the light all honeyed, and how hollow the body of the owl, messenger of the underworld I always listen for through night windows, all these words metaphor for *Braille*, I think: poet I would be running her fingers tenderly along a feather, barb and quill writing this strange and mothered air.

MIGRATION CORRIDORS

Environmental protection, what they do is a
disgrace: every week they come out with new
regulations.
                                —Trump, *Fox News Sunday*

THE ELK TRAVEL from places higher than ours. They step
down from crags and rotted granite to our mountain meadow
to graze, then vanish for winter into montane valleys below,
their journeys spurred when the wild aster bloom and foxtails
cling to the dogs—a windless dispersal I love, feeding next
spring and its sparse bloomings.

I often thought that migration must come over you
like sleep, like something holy, like the light of a sun or a
mountain's half-light or the rose light of half-turned trees, the
way sleep, here, on this land I want to call my own, settles
into the owl pellets I find, into the slow swallow of tooth and
nail, into the deep felt of lichen and the drowsy grass I lay in,
where blue harebells bend, a singing in the conifer trees as
far away as childhood, as the pine sounding like a dark sea
outside my mother's back porch, me, a girl, listening.

Years now, Leonard and I have watched the elk cross the
wide meadow to the north of us—"Their migration path," my
neighbors say. "We're in the middle of it." Or we've watched
their white rumps vanish into the east woods, the dogs at their
heels darting over a rise we can't quite see past until, suddenly,
a whole river of elk rush back and we cower against a tree,

those prow-necked travelers passing by us on their altitudinal migrations, once eighty we counted before dawn—no birds yet singing, but owl murmurs and scarce crickets.

"Look," says Joseph, my tree cutter from Kansas. June, he chainsaws my aspen for fire mitigation again, my never-ending "standing dead." He holds up his droid with its shaky image of what looks to be a thin and sickly deer. It hunches at the barbed wire fence that carves my and my neighbors' 40 acre parcels out of the heart of what was once the Dilly Ranch, a 2000-acre solitary expanse of bunch grass and civil-engineered holding ponds for snow melt and scarce summer rains. Though the ranch has long been sub-divided, nearby ranchers still herd their cattle through, a leasing arrangement good for cabin owners like me because of agriculture tax breaks, despite cow pies big as garbage lids that sometimes pile at the front porch step.

I can barely make out the pixels.

"A pronghorn. That's what my girlfriend says."

Pronghorn. No way. This high, we are simply refuge to the longhorns and angus cows of neighbor ranchers and to the mule deer and the seasonal elk and, occasionally, to glue factory horses hauled up from flatland ranches and abandoned inside our cattle grates to wander bell-hoofed through the summer until they vanish—these meadows too far above the Arkansas Valley and its scattered bands of pronghorns for a single stray to venture.

Pronghorns. I look them up online. They once outnumbered the 30 million bison that thundered through the prairie lowlands west of the Mississippi to the Rockies and beyond, the bison that Buffalo Bill slaughtered 4000 of in two years, ancestors to the stuffed effigies hanging over the bars at *Ted's Montana Grill.* The pronghorns, I discover, were the prey of an American cheetah, a *Miracinonyx inexpectatus* (wonderful! unexpected!), its fossil remains dating back 3.2

million years ago until its extinction at the end of the last Ice
Age, this cheetah credited evolutionarily for the 70 mile an
hour spurts of speed of these fastest mammals in the Western
Hemisphere. For 6000 years, the pronghorns have traveled
the Path of the Pronghorn from the Upper Green River Valley
of Wyoming to Jackson Hole one hundred miles away, this
path one of North America's longest remaining mammal
migration corridors.

   Migration Corridors. I look that up, too. In the prose of
science, migration corridors are "habitats that follow natural
landmarks and allow seasonal migration between summer and
winter grazing and breeding grounds." I think of the summer
cows wandering their long revolutions between Eightmile
creek and the homesteader ruins in the spring below the cabin
and the glory holes above the valley I pass everywhere, their
cow paths I walk worn laterally around our steepest hills and
shallowest gullies. Sparked by temperature change, snowfall,
a failing of light maybe or some seismic shift within a spatial
dimension oblivious to our human senses, so wildlife, too,
have followed in their migrations their own global "paths of
least resistance."

   But why do I care about this migration and the scant
possibility that those blurry pixels Joseph saved on his Iphone
really belong to a pronghorn? Because of the same changes
that lead me to fallen birds and their tiny bones? Because my
mother flew from her Ohio trees and beloved sisters, from
my brother and the grandchildren who grew up with her, to
here, to me, her middle child she barely knows? Or because
our identical daughters, Kitty and Mira, have splintered apart:
Kitty to care for rescue birds in Aspen and teach children
her love of nature and Mira to the middle of Chicago in a
high rise above a church and a YMCA with her soon-to-be
ex-boyfriend who watched drug deals "go down" from their
balcony until Mira fled to another country? Or because this
year we watched the plain pine box of my Jewish brother-in

law descend into a hole, sweat on our shirts as we took turns spilling dirt over him—sad emissaries at the door of his far travels, *katabasa?* Or because of the migrant children we now take from their parents who pass our southern borders?

I remember late nights driving down the lane past the aspens' yellow leaves, elk startling at the edge of our headlights, every bird and animal, I realize now, arriving by some means of migration, whether steered by star, by water, by what else I do not know. I think of my mother migrating here, of my Russian mother-in-law, (I've forgotten how many years dead now), at ten, walking with her family across the Russian tundra after the pogroms, everything it seemed lost, the river gypsies kidnapping her sister for crossing fare, and of that migration corridor she and her family followed until finally she settled here, close to the acres homesteaded by her father in Wyoming—her son, my husband, here, now, because his mother could find refuge here, and our daughters, her granddaughters, here, who in defiance of the political, caption their pictures on Facebook, *Immigrant Descendants.*

A website I find, called, appropriately, "listsofeverything," lists 47 migratory species of fish, mammals, and birds around the world, which just doesn't seem enough. And then I see that it condenses eighteen hundred migrating bird species into just one general "Birds" category and leaves out other species like the ten thousand Green Darner dragonflies that a professional hawk counter I read about once tracked over a single ridge in Duluth, Minnesota and the one thousand kestrels, too, that winged past him. And there is no mention of the maelstrom of miller moths that mount on the plains in summer in such numbers that our Denver newspaper warns us of their mountain migration, how they will barge at the window screens, bang at my reading lamp until I find their brittle exoskeletons littering the floor by morning.

Still, I am struck by the wonder of this migration list and all that it does not name, that any moment, countless sentient beings, animal and human, circle this earth in hope, whether grounded, submerged or aerial, and engage in some primal encoding to fulfill this world's one directive, what only my mother keeps telling me she does not want to do: *Exist*.

Dean, a cabin neighbor still with movie star looks, and his retired school teacher wife, once drove up on an ATV from their cabin in the small valley below us, where hummingbirds swarm their feeders and perch on their fingers to feed, to warn us with a grin to watch out for "Rufus." Rufus turns out to be the plucky little Rufous hummingbird in iridescent rusty armor that propels itself each spring by a four-inch wing span along the Pacific flyway from Mexico to Canada. It returns en route in July to our little red sugar feeder and its oblivious cadre of broad-tailed and ruby-throated hummingbirds, all ripe for the dive-bombing of a *Rufus*. It's one of many migrations I wait here for. Late winters, the blue birds from as far away as Texas and Mexico swoop across the meadow's mustard yellow grass to nest on our porch beams where they nested last year and the years before. And the elk return, which 10,000 years ago crossed a vanished land bridge before the time of the ancient Ute Indians' own migration each summer from the plains to Pike's Peak, their *Shining Mountain* we can glimpse from our front porch. Summers, the woods fill with bird song I cannot name after silent winters of just hawk and crow, turkey vulture, the occasional stellar jay dispelling the snow's hush—existence, as I have learned to know and love it here, returned.

Kitty works at the Aspen Center for Environmental Studies where she feeds owls anchored on her gloved arm and listens to the crack of mice skulls. She tells me that loss of habitat is the primal threat to any species, and though there is no immediate threat of "migration extinction," the migrants themselves are diminishing due to destructed habitat and construction barriers like dams and fences and presidential walls and beloved cabins. And I realize, too, on 40-acre parcels where now a pronghorn travels, my fellow suburbanite migrants and I are culpable for habitat destruction and its threat of diminishment. We have divided wide corridors of land into fenced parcels and built small beloved cabins or 10,000 square foot executive hunting lodges where elk, deer and now a single pronghorn travel. When Joey, our border collie mutt, barks our arrival to the cabin the entire way down the lane and sends that river of elk into a rushing panic, he is a domesticated deterrent to migration for which I alone am responsible.

I keep thinking about the word Kitty used, "diminishment." I read of the bee colonies' demise, yet still bees buzz at our bluebeards, Joey in the suburbs trying to snap them from the air. But what do we remember of a decade ago or of a childhood ago, of how many bees gone from how many wild flowers we don't remember? Or the gossamer of spiders lost? A few springs ago, I found a hundred miner bees unhived in the winter spill of our yard, *a hundred little deaths*, I told Mother, and how Leonard each summer since counts the scarce bees hovering at our blossoms.

"Do you remember those hives of bees that Dad tended on the farm?" I ask Mother. "How the bees circled Dad in the smoke?" She smiles at me, not really hearing.

"Where are the bees?" Leonard keeps asking.

Highway 191, a stretch of barbed wire-enclosed roadway in Wyoming intersected by subdivisions, cuts through the Path of the Pronghorn. It has long exacerbated the pronghorns' ancient migration path through the natural geological "bottle-neck" there at Trapper's Point, site of charcoal pits and bones dating back 7,000 years ago. "The earliest evidence of humans hunting pronghorn in the world," the archeologists tell us. There, each year, since the highway's construction, hundreds of pronghorns have met their death, driven by the same instinctual urge of their ancestors to migrate when our own human ancestors hunted with stone projectiles.

I am so weary of the news of our animal killing. Yet there is good news, too, I find out: since the Path of the Pronghorn was recognized by the U.S. Forest Service in 2008 as the first federally designated wildlife corridor, the Wyoming Department of Transportation has paid millions to construct wildlife overpasses and underpasses along the bottleneck. Videos show me images of pronghorns walking the manmade bridges.

Good, yes, but I can't help to think that this particular migration corridor has both scientific and tourist industry cachet. What about the less spectacular corridors and aerial migration flyways for the animals and birds that confront more than 82,000 fracking wells reportedly drilled in Colorado (and more now) by *Environment America* since 2005? Or what about, as *The Washington Post* calls it, "Death by Solar Farm"—the 300,000 mirrors on 3500 acres in California that incinerate mid-air the luckless birds passing overhead? Or the "hundreds upon hundreds" of butterflies, our vanishing Monarchs included, said to be attracted to the solar farm's light, then burnt, their carcasses scattered amid the mirrors? The solar farm workers nickname the birds "streamers" for the "little puff of smoke" they emit as they die through "solar flex," a term for exposure to temperatures over 800 degrees Fahrenheit. One group of federal investigators, observing what the article calls the "phenomena," estimated spotting one streamer every two minutes—hawks, coots, cowbirds, sparrows, warblers, owls, hummingbirds, heron, teals—a total of 71 different bird species turned to smoke.

Here in Teller County, the old Cripple Creek & Victor Gold Mining Company (CC &V) now Newmont Mining company reminds us on its website—"Living a Mining Heritage"—that it continues to maw at Cresson Mine, now an open pit mining operation where once sixty thousand ounces of gold were discovered in a natural "vug" in the earth. It's this open-pit mine that piles "over burden"—the gold-less waste rock that can't be used—at such a rate it delays the very rising of the sun and disrupts how many unknown migration paths along the now decimated Grassy Valley and its 45 "typical wildlife species observed to be present," as reported in CC&V's original Permit, filed before the Cresson Project Mine Life Extension 2 began. In addition to the mine, the development of a new private shooting facility continues on 147 acres of ranch land along County Rd 81, once owned by a working cow ranch called *The Lazy-S* and now owned by the mining company. The original developers of the shooting facility promised that "Perimeter fencing of the entire range site will be of smooth wire with spacing to allow migrating Elk calves room to crawl under the fence"—as if baby elk in migration with their moms would venture into a fenced shooting enclave built for high powered rifles, which will include a 10,000 square foot "Future Club House" facility, ten shooting ranges, a 28 foot high observation tower, assorted gazebos for picnicking, restrooms, pedestrian benches, and a maintenance shed.

Not so long ago, to little public brouhaha—I feel myself warming to this subject—the U.S. Fish and Wildlife Service finalized a new policy affecting the interpretation of the Endangered Species Act of 1973, specifically the interpretation of the phrase "significant portion" in the original definition of "endangered species": "any species which is in danger of extinction throughout all or a significant portion of its range." The designation of "significant" now applies only if the portion of range afflicted means the threat of extinction for the species as a whole, not just for that particular geographic population, a change that according to the Center for Biological Diversity "eviscerates the key requirement that species need not be at risk of extinction everywhere before they can be protected." In other words, if my little bully *Rufus* disappears from these meadows at 9600 feet where it and other hummingbirds have migrated for thousands of years or if the elk in late summer fail to travel down from the crags and rotted granite above us because we have blocked their flyways and corridors and created the habitat fragmentation *Plos Biology* warns us of, we would have no cause for alarm or recourse under the revised Endangered Species Act as long as these generational travelers continued to live and breed in lands and even countries far away from us.

But even that bad news was in another era. Today's Senate hearings undertake the "modernization" of the Endangered Species Act, those who would undo it in our current administration claiming it "hijacks" progress. I must wonder what consequences of policy change await us that are as unknown to us now as were the installation of solar mirrors for the very best of "green" reasons that drop those charred streamers minute by minute from the sky. I read in the newspapers' litanies of other policy changes and wonder does it matter if the wolves, brought back by the Endangered Species Act and trembling at our Colorado borders, can be shot now with their cubs in their dens or that these same wolves may one day be perpetuated only as hybrids in sanctuaries, presented to tourists as "eco-features" behind wire fences?

Mira, my ex-Chicago daughter, tells me that many of the inner-city kids she worked with didn't think about wild animals. They had never seen them, the city they lived in so long ago disrupting migration corridors and flyways that some children instead talked about hurting the hungry stray dogs and cats they saw slinking through city shadows. Some children of the Roaring Fork Valley, born to the immigrants who followed their own migration corridors across our man-made borders and whom we threaten to deport now and separate from their children, cry in fear to my owl-wielding Kitty, "You have brown eyes, too. Will you have to leave?"

I feel some comfort learning what I do about migration, that patterns way beyond our understanding still exist after hundreds of thousands of years and that those patterns continue, both human and animal. The pronghorn captured on Joseph's android, its ancestors once decimated to just 20,000 a hundred years ago, reminds me of the power of "dispersal," (not to be confused with migration, I'm warned), when an animal moves to another habitat outside its birth range and, perhaps by doing so, increases biodiversity and lessens, in the long run, its species' chance of extinction. I still remember the week I spent in Grand Lake teaching for a writer's group when I saw for the first time a moose stepping ungainly, majestic, over the borders of Stillwater Pass, its antlers flowering on its otherworldly head, its calf slipping under the fence rail to follow. Now my straw-bale house neighbor Kathy, who used to hike over just to hug the exposed timber posts of our cabin, tells me that she has seen not one moose, but two near the small wetlands of Cripple Creek.

Come fall, if we are lucky, the elk will stand again at the edge of our high beams like silvered effigies poised on the brink of flight. We'll worry over their diminishing, over a wall, over the cries of brown-eyed children, over grieving mothers, over birds and bees and spiders so lost to us that we no longer even know to count them. And all through the winter, I will rub my fingers along the aspens' paper bark, along the black scars where, years, the elk have rubbed their velvet free, stepped out from the timbers to rut amid ruins and glory holes, ghosts at dawn and dusk I keep listening for, when the wind passing over the gold mines stills and the softer valleys below glitter.

FUNNEL WEAVERS

THIS MORNING, a single strand of silk shines above our loft railing in the eastern light. Heartless, I know, I used to knock it down with a feather duster each time I returned to the cabin and awakened to *Aurora*, to Homer's *rosy-fingered* dawn, and saw that motionless spider web, *dragline* it's called, dangling from the timber beams. But now it stays.

I have yet to see the spider that the dragline carries through that Keatsian *"tender eye-dawn of aurorean love,"* and even if I did now, I would have to fly downstairs to the cabinet beneath the sink for the jelly jam "spider jar" Leonard keeps handy in both our suburban and mountain kitchens, despite his repeated accusation that I am an "intrepid spider murderer."

"Slaughterer of Thousands," he likes to call me.

It seems I am writing about spiders today because Leonard and Mother have told me that I should not write about the western "land grab" I read about in the *New York Times*. I shared with Mother, visiting with us at the cabin, the revelation that with the inception of a nonprofit organization called *American Lands Council*, there had been an orchestrated attempt by states, including Colorado, to turn public lands over to state control in the name of "better" stewardship of our national resources, or, as in the words of ALC's mission statement, "to ensure better access, better health, AND better productivity"—the capital letters and emphasis on "AND" all theirs. Meaning, I am beginning to understand, drilling.

Mother, who I have discovered prefers chit chat over the political, chuckles and says, "Better stick to spiders."

In Chicago, during Mira's last summer there, her boyfriend took us for a late-night drink in the John Hancock Observatory bar, 1000 feet above the "Magnificent Mile." The city lights at our feet wove an unknown galaxy, the moon floating barely above us like a cheesecloth imposter we could almost touch. Unbeknownst to me then, to any motherly instinct I might pride myself on having, he was soon to be my daughter's ex, Mira fleeing to teach English in another country, though I stood at the JC Penney counter with them not long before she left, gazing at rings and offering this boyfriend I later learned had hurt her two small diamonds from my own refurbished engagement ring.

Looking through the midnight drinkers so ghostly in the reflective glass that night, I knew none of this nor of the spiders that can fly ninety-five stories into the air to spin their webs on steel ledges, to lower themselves in the wind and rise again, this fact of rising I think important now, metaphoric in some way I have yet to figure out. Instead, I pressed my hands against the skyscraper's broad panes, thinking of those at the top of the burning Trade Towers perched on broken windowsills—that vista of lights beneath me, beneath them like some far heaven turned under.

I have never been one to scream out at spiders, though I must admit I have, as Leonard claims, killed them with the whisk of a broom, especially when our daughters were young— our suburban basement a Jackson Pollock canvas of dusky, half-dollar sized spiders saved by Leonard (*Black Widow? Brown Recluse?* I kept asking him) wandering its winter walls. Occasionally, Leonard still bursts from the basement door to get his spider jar, and in any number of contortionist's postures, carefully tips the biggest spider in, no matter how innocuous or venomous, to shake it outside on the bushes, frost or none.

Last night in bed, when I tried to talk about something other than spiders, Leonard explained to me, "You are a more lyrical writer," when I explained to him what *The New York Times* column said about this "Sagebrush Rebellion" to turn public lands over to the control of states and, ominously, prosperous oil companies. When I looked up the American Lands Council's website with its banners of leaf-kicking grandsons and *Our Team* bios of cattle-ranch board members, I could see that it belied its association with what the column called the "conservative" American Legislative Exchange Council. The ALEC (its logo *Limited Government-Free Markets-Federalism*) helped draft what the American Lands Council calls the "model legislation" it shopped around Washington to curry favor for the land grab.

But, "aye," as my Shakespeare-loving Leonard would say, "there's the rub." Members of the Exxon Mobile Corporation, Energy Future Holdings, and Peabody Energy helped draft this legislation.

"Oh, my god," I said to Leonard as he handed me a poem of mine he found on the desk. (*This is really good*, he said, *just as good as all those other poems out there I can't understand*.) "It's the fracking!"

All night, it has rained. Not the mythic rain of floods conjured by gods because of some human flaw of too much knowing, but a fine rain, our rain gauge recording over 5 inches this month, more than I once saw for an entire year when every day brought us deeper into drought—the earth cracked into scales, the aspen leaves stunted into mice hearts, into our hearts.

Kitty and Mira were eleven when the towers fell. I remember how I worried over them, (*how many nights*) lying in their beds beneath those stars that wheeled so asymmetrically, so unknown nightly over us: silent the winter nights beneath the stars, silent the moon, Mira, who would one day leave us for that far country, holding onto me in the mornings before I left for work, weeping, *don't go, don't go.*

How little I know of my daughter's life, of her loves now. I study the pictures she posts on Facebook. She stands in the ruins of a country far from me in a place of blossom and warm rain. I think about the cold hands and the straight wooden yardstick of my mother, my skin like a length of spring muslin she pinned to me, what I see now I have pinned to my own daughters, still not understanding what it means to be a mother loving a daughter already leaving, already left.

"I am in love," Mira texts her twin and posts videos of a boy she kisses in a field of horses while I count the days to her returning home.

"Returning only to despair," Mira tells me, blaming me for my wanting her.

In Chaucer's *The Squire's Tale*, the Squire agrees to tell another tale of love—his lines referenced by arachnologists, spider lovers—everywhere:

> *Sore wondren some on cause of thonder,*
> *On ebb and floud, on gossomer, and mist.*

Spiders, it turns out, produce multiple types of spider silk, some sticky, some not. Gossamer is their finest silk, a protein fiber that spiders, especially spiderlings, use in "ballooning," in leaving: the baby spider in a headstand spinning out a single strand of silk from its abdomen to lasso the wind and be carried skyward, sometimes to altitudes miles above us, the "ballooners" finally settling down everywhere in the coolness of evening toward earth or, sometimes, on the ledges of a sky rise or, sometimes, in a far field of wet blossom where a daughter swallowing a single seed can break a mother's heart.

Metaphor, I tell my dear mother, the stuff of poetry. And spiders.

Mother leans back in the rocking chair. She too is afraid Mira will not return, as I did not return to her, as she is afraid of her own leaving of this world, though she cannot say that, and, instead, insists the opposite. *Katabasa* in mythology, I explain to Mother, is a sinking into the underworld. For it to be a true Katabasis and not simply a death, there must be an *Anabasis*, a rising up, like those spiders on the high rise, I tell Mother, when I stood there with Mira and her boyfriend looking out a window to that fallen heaven, to that new world of the fallen.

Mother reminds me that, for her, there will be no return, no blossoms, no spot on this earth I might weep into.

"Don't cry for me," she says, and I promise her, like the good daughter I want to be.

L. Turnball, a British scholar, estimated in his 1973 paper, *Ecology of the True Spiders (Araneomorphae)*, that throughout this earth, there are on average 130.8 spiders per square meter. When I turn to look at Mother, I see not one spider web, but two in the doorframe behind her.

"You are always within three feet of a spider," I tell her of the old wives' tale.

"Oh," Mother says, half-laughing. "I'm getting the creeps just stepping anywhere."

Pliny the Eldest, a Roman Historian and Encyclopedist, who died trying to save family members from the Mt. Vesuvius eruption that destroyed Pompeii, wrote: *"In the year that L. Paulus and C. Marcellus were consuls it rained wool."*

Imagine, I say to Mother, how many spiders back then must have birthed how many hundreds of spiderlings for that much silk to be ballooning in the wind for Pliny to even think of that metaphor for gossamer. Imagine it: untold fathoms drifting to earth in the eventide of a lost world. *Fils de la Vierge*, the French call gossamer, *Our Lady's Threads.* "Diminishment," I think, that term I keep remembering, on how everything so slowly deteriorates that we don't even comprehend the vanishing.

But I don't tell Mother this, who prefers her chit chat to not just the political, but to the religious and to the deteriorating, too, except her own.

Rain spills down enough this morning that the ground we once drilled through to dig a well whole stories underneath us blackens beneath the dogs' and my feet. *Rotted granite*, the geologists call this soil—harbinger of the gold that the glory holes I stumble across promised. In another century, miners in Cripple Creek and Victor drilled into those cavities of gold they called *vugs*, gold flakes the size of fingernails buried deep beneath this earth in caverns just like those caverns of the mythic worlds and their long underground rivers of forgetting, heroes, not like me, journeying into the lands of the dead and then returning wiser in katabasis to those who still love them to make those loved ones wiser, too.

Monday, Leonard and I meet with our lawyer to update our wills, living and temporal, to name our daughters successors in case we should both die, as my mother has named me successor, our lives as cyclical as the moon's or the serpent's eating its own tail. Before my mother moved here, she became almost mythic during our thirty-some-year parting, a woman from my childhood I could not sometimes define except by legend and lore. I sit next to her at the doctor's now or at the bank and sense when this woman who seemed so indominable is hurt, when she feels herself replaced, the nurses speaking to me as if she were a child.

"I sit there like dumb dumb Dora hearing nothing," she complains to me, this mythic mother I once writ so large as a child now this tiny woman I barely know, tiny woman my mother says I am not to write of, to name. But do.

"Well, you left Grandma," my wandering Mira says over the phone as we discuss her return and I remember my mother's stories of driving 24 hours from Ohio across country to see my sister in Kansas and then me, the eastern Colorado wind ripping at her car door.

"So hard," Mother always said, though I hardly knew it then.

The day the Towers fell and the world changed, I like to think I would have said something—a word, *snow, I love you*, the names of our daughters—before standing on the window ledge, the wind snuffling at trousers and dress skirts, the pieces of others drifting upward, their burnt shoes opening their black mouths. I think what haunts me about that day are the similarities: the white and blue collared workers (soon to be dead) of a day, of a building, as stationed and dutiful as I once was beneath a corporate fluorescent glare while the world fell, and my daughters cried.

"You know," Leonard says, "the federal government has been leasing lands to oil companies for decades now. So, what's the difference?" Annoyingly, Leonard is right: a report by Congressional Research Service cites U.S. Bureau of Land Management data of over 72 million acres of oil and gas leases in federal areas.

So, what is the difference?

My *New York Times* column argues that despite the claims that closer to home management would better protect our national heirlooms and provide relief to an overburdened national government, the cost of management would actually drive states to auction off land. Highest bidders would surely include private corporations, which could result in a "proliferation of locked gates and no-trespassing signs."

And fracking?

It's hard, I tell Mother, not to start the mental gymnastics with the news that the BLM had thousands of outstanding bids to drill on public land or that Trump and his Interior Secretary now, despite their insistence that public lands will not be sold off even as the boundaries of National Monuments are "shrink-wrapped," call for expanded oil and gas drilling on public land and the removal of "bureaucratic impediments," like the laws that prevent harm to our national parks.

But, as my mother would point out, I digress from the chit chat. I am supposed to be writing about spiders, the funnel weaver spider, to be exact. I remember the man I met on the trail to Mount Sneffels in the San Juan Mountains who, pardon me, "sniffed" when I told him about our little forty acres of heaven nestled here in Teller County between the backside of Pike's Peak and Nipple Mountain we shadow in.

"I always hated that part of the state," he said, looking out at the lush San Juan tapestry of snowmelt streams and wildflower plethora. "So barren."

The first time I saw the tunnels of the funnel weaver in the grass, I thought them like old ear trumpets and I wanted something different, something better in this little heaven I had bought than these most common of grass spiders and their most common of webs—something like the wolf spider, *Lycosa*, towing its mob of spiderlings piggy-back, or the golden orb weaver, like Arachne, mortal weaver in Greek myth, looming its web with "scenes of wayward joys in heaven." But my land, my little piece of cattle ranch, call it "agricultural," is a utilitarian land, good, I suppose, for only utilitarian spiders. And atheist mothers. And reluctant returning daughters.

Wild fires from the drought of this decade's start, which once covered the sun in a gauze of smoke, are mythic now. Crevices and gullies ran fresh with rain this last spring and what we once could only imagine to be wetlands is wet again. Our own dams and berms dug by the unrisen dead filled this spring with snowmelt our dogs could swim through. The first flowers, pasque flowers, returned, too, mythic or metaphoric: *Easter flower, wind flower,* as they're nicknamed, their downy seeds as beaten as we are by wind.

A few summers past marked 50 years of the Wilderness Act. Its inception began here in Colorado in response to the Federal Government's proposal to flood Echo Park, a canyon in the heart of Dinosaur National Monument where 149 million-year-old dinosaur fossils exist amidst 1200-year-old petroglyphs and the spawning grounds of 5 million-year-old fish named Razorback Sucker and the Bonytail, considered North America's most endangered species of fish.

In the years after, when we should be celebrating what is considered to be "one of America's greatest conservation achievements," with its preservation of 109 million acres of public land, how ironic I think that the Trump administration would ransack these very same National parks, prioritizing drilling on even the most fragile and rare places of our world, like the Arctic National Wildlife Refuge where polar bears and brown bears co-exist and 200 bird species migrate to and from every backyard and wild place in the United States.

Edward O. Wilson, a Pulitzer prize winning biologist, once said, "When you thrust a shovel into the soil or tear off a piece of coral, you are, godlike, cutting through an entire world"—this true whether that shovelful be national monument land, agricultural land, or the "barren" land of an old mountain cattle ranch where solitary wildflowers stagger beneath the bunchgrass you love.

Sometime soon, I will write my sister, and even my brother, whose careless remark about leaving her drove our mother from Ohio, how hard all this is: the shade of our mother I accompany to the underworlds of her imaginings, my seed-filled daughter and her grieving, and this once godly earth we keep cutting into. Joseph Campbell, as I tell my mythology students, says that mortality underpins everything and is what finally gives us suffering. And yet if we accept that, if we see what I keep calling *diminishment* as a natural cycle, a rebirth, then we can find some kind of transcendence to save us. Someday, I suppose, we'll tell our children's children our own myths, how whole buildings once rose then fell, dust like snow floating up from the earth, quiet like last ash, like last bone, the last ticking of a thousand wrist watches—metaphor for an old world and the creation of a new one they won't understand—settling on the rooftops.

This morning, a soft spread of cloud, like spring cloud, promises more rain, *female rain*, the Navajo call it, what will come softly, like a daughter home, or a mother far from it, and bead the tiny webs of this eight-eyed funnel spider, its radiating sheet webs in the grass I have long walked over suddenly visible—blurred, haloed, a night's wetness caught like child's tears.

Gossamer, I'll call it.

On Intla: Snow that has Drifted Indoors

I still feel the need of some imperishable bliss.
—Wallace Stevens, *Harmonium*

THE WORD INTLA IS SUPPOSEDLY one of the fifty, or even a hundred, of the words the Inuit Indians of the Arctic use for snow. I recited them once to my mother, ill and sad on the eve of a winter solstice. How we marveled at the beauty of these words, their corporeality, the very fleshiness of snow we could feel again against our tongues—those far Ohio snows, winters with my father and brother and sister, how young we were, the blades of our skates scouring the dark ice of our winter pond as we made our great loops again and again beneath the gray world, snow in the air glittering, in our hair glittering: *klin—remembered snow, naklin—forgotten snow, snow that blinds you—krotla.*

Last winter, I drove through freezing fog to reach our cabin, a great slick of it settled over Highway 24 through Ute Pass toward Divide. There was no *ontla* yet, *no snow on objects*, but atmospheric icing, water droplets in the air freezing on everything they touched. And then the rime formed—hard or soft, I don't know—ice, it seemed, encasing everything this winter fog touched, the white tufts of it battened to every frail stem I drove past, every last hanging leaf of the past year, as if some merciful god I could believe in had dipped the pillaged world into bridal white, even the gas tank at the gas station covered in a bearded frost—*hiryla, snow in beards*—on its "windward side," what I'm told, *points to the wind.*

You see, it was the day the two French terrorists attacked the *Charlie Hebdo* or the day two thousand Nigerians were slaughtered by a militant extremist group that kidnaps schoolgirls. I drove past Pikes Peak where those ancient Ute Indians once migrated and believed *Ta-Wa-ah-Gath*, *Sun Mountain Sitting Big*, *Shining Mountain*, to be their nascent world—their Great Spirit out of a hole in the sky showering down enough snow and ice, *tlapinti, snow that falls quickly,* for a whole new glittering world that I, too, wanted.

Of course, the EPA had come out with its annual report, too, and it looked grim. The report looks at conditions of a specific environmental area over a span of time that seem to indicate enduring climate changes. The indicators of change include the predictable like greenhouse gas emissions, global temperatures, ocean heat, but the lesser-known ones, too, that surprised me, like Lyme disease, ragweed pollen, bird wintering ranges, and the leaf and bloom dates. And, of course, snow: the fall and breadth and depth of it. Certainly, according to this report, not enough for that new world the Utes searched for with each migration.

Wallace Stevens said, "One must have a mind of winter" and "been cold a long time":

not to think
Of any misery in the sound of the wind,
In the sound of a few leaves.

This spring, I am to speak on a writer's panel about the spiritual memoir and I'm wondering how cold I am. "Do we build or blow up bridges between the faith community and the private realm of the spiritual?" we'll ask ourselves. Or "what craft choices do we make, especially describing the exposition of insight and the drama of awakening?" And, finally, "are we 'spiritualized' by writing these books, especially when we, the ex-religious ones,"—or me, the never religious one—"attempt the peril of translating ineffable experience into narrative and essay?"

Leonard, when I tell him of my spring quest, has, of course, something to say.

"You and the 'spiritual'?" He pauses to savor the moment. "Kind of a complete contradiction, wouldn't you say?"

Ineffable experience. I do wonder what that means. Exactly. Is it when I think of my father, as Leonard reminds me I am ought to do, left behind in that country graveyard I played in as a child, buried in a tiny plot of earth in a place called Murdoch where the grass never would grow, and now, as if I dreamed awake, he's walking toward us once more from the far fields—soybean or the hay we baled each late summer— sweat black on the rim of his straw hat, a whole continent of shadow, of hide hair and chaff across the belly of his shirt, and his soul still half-light, still potter's clay?

Chiup, snow that makes haloes.

"Reality is a cliché from which we escape by metaphor," Stevens said, perhaps this language of poetry easier for me than the language of the spiritual. By the time I reached Divide, the rime had disappeared and the frozen fog that iced the air laid below me like a great and faraway sea I might forget. At the cattle crossing to the old Dilly Ranch, the southern sun above the Sangre de Cristo Mountains blinded me and I remembered how glad I was to be there, calling the mountains *Blood of Christ,* as I had heard them called, and the hollows in the snow patches scattered across our high mountain meadow *sun cups,* though I knew them to be *ablation hollows,* depressions (metaphor, you see) formed in the snow by sun or by constant wind. Our wind, "which is the sound of the land," as Stevens said,

> …blowing in the same bare place
> For the listener, who listens in the snow.

I live mostly far below this cabin in a suburb that can feel like the epicenter of disaster. A *community of faith*, I think I'll call it that I don't belong to, so distant from this solitary place of wind and sometimes snow that I always migrate to, driving past the geological unconformities and faults of a mountain made by shifting tectonic plates millions of years ago, along a highway where I can still imagine Indians traveling to breathe in the breath of Great Spirits bubbling through water.

Holy, they said.

Krikaya, snow mixed with breath.

Down below on the plains, my community college students wear black lipstick and write of running into smiling men who pull shotguns from their coats and shoot their friends dead. Or they wear sweaty track uniforms to class and write, "I found it boring," when locked down in classrooms, awaiting the cavalry of police who would lead them past school lunchrooms and libraries left again to the dead.

And there is always Columbine.

"You let your daughters go to Columbine?" a friend recently marveled to me and I thought of the bomb threats I had forgotten all these years since Kitty and Mira attended Columbine, despite my protestations to the contrary on the day of the shootings when they were in the second grade, locked for "safety" in the nearby elementary school's chained auditorium. *Never*, I remember saying. One year, Kitty and Mira told me, when they, of course, attended Columbine, the principal, who had not yet retired and ever since Columbine was forced to run a gauntlet of news interviews and stories with each new shooting across the country, dove behind a podium during a school assembly because a balloon burst. What bridge of faith did I have then, sending them there, when my own community college students, even seventeen years later, semester after semester, still write, *I was there?*

Mortla, snow mounded on the dead.

I admit I am no Bible scholar, but sometimes I'll open a random page of my great great, possibly great, grandmother's crusty black *Holy Bible*, bible that I confess should be my born-again sister's, with its beautiful fading ink inscription to *Elizabeth Smith on Christmas 1881* from her sister, a name I can't quite make out. There, amid the tiny tattered bookmarks of Elizabeth and her tiny tickets of prayer, *The peace of God, which passeth all understanding*, and the schedule for an 1887 prayer meeting at Mt. Auburn Presbyterian Church, and this Bible's recording of family deaths and births, even my father's own, I read what happenstance brings me. *For we know in part*, the First Epistle to the Corinthians tells me this day, *and we prophesy in part*.

I don't yet understand this. Exactly.

Last night, my mother spoke of snow again. Metaphor, you see, those poetics I can understand. *Cold*, she said, winters feeding our cattle in Ohio, and, *heavy*, dragging the hay bales across the barn loft, cutting the baling twine free, and the hay scattering through the loft window like *bluwid, snow shaken down from objects in the wind*, I the girl child waiting below for the beloved mother to climb the ladder down: how good it felt, running my bared fingers through the cleaning frost, the skim of trough ice.

"I just don't understand why I'm here," Mother said at dinner, again, with her customary half-chuckle. "I don't mean *here*, but, here in this world, now."

Tlayopi, snow drifts you fall into and die.

I imagine all I love here at this cabin at 9600 feet—coyotes yipping toward dawn, the chirr of house wren outside the window, Leonard's warm breath at night against my neck— as if it might be lost tomorrow. Metaphor, or prophecy, I think, from which we discover those unknown connections that bind self with *other* that perhaps allow us to experience momentarily that completeness that Paul the Apostle speaks of, *we who see through a glass darkly* [and cannot yet] *speak in the tongues of men or angel.* Perils of the spiritual memoir, I guess, my mother counting down the number of cousins who didn't show up at the annual Christmas lunch last year—she, too, of course, missing, because of her own migrations.

Of course, the FJ Cruiser stuck. Teller County averages only sixty inches of snow each year, a far cry from the 180 inches of snow of a ski resort like Aspen. At our old "banana-belt" cattle ranch, most of our snow is wind-blown, baring summer cattle droppings and uneaten brome grass. By the time I swung around the last curve of the snow-patched two-wheel lane to our cabin, I had forgotten *slimtla, snow that is crusted on top but soft underneath* and barreled right into a drift of it, though *drift* seems like the wrong word for this snow that my neighbor Tandy, ex-pat from suburbia who married Dave, the mountain cattle rancher we lease our land to, warned me of years ago.

"Like concrete," she said. "All that melting and freezing. You'll stick until spring."

In the hour I spent digging out, after hiking the mile to the cabin for the hand shovel—"uh, a quarter mile," claims Leonard, who was, of course, not there for the walking nor the shoveling—I had plenty of time to think about real snow, even in the face of a National Climatic Data Center report that said "the globally-averaged temperature across land and ocean surfaces was...the highest on record for December since records began in 1880." Increased greenhouse gas, a "positive climate forcing" or warming effect, the thinning of Arctic Ice, a decrease in snow cover of thirty-five thousand square miles per year since 1972, more rain than snow fall, and even the too-early blooming of lilacs and honeysuckle, according to computer-generated models—these are the alarming consequences, EPA warns us, of climate-driven ecosystem changes that could happen too quickly for the plants and animals in that system to adapt.

Frederick Karl, biographer of Franz Kafka, describes the *Kafkaesque* as when:

> *you enter a surreal world in which all your control patterns, all your plans, the whole way in which you have configured your own behavior, begins to fall to pieces, when you find yourself against a force that does not lend itself to the way you perceive the world. You don't give up, you don't lie down and die. What you do is struggle against this with all of your equipment, with whatever you have. But of course, you don't stand a chance.*

Hardly spiritual, I know. A few years ago, when even *tla, ordinary snow,* in the north crevices of our rocks had melted, I remember standing on the deck of our cabin before leaving for a few weeks to the MFA residency I taught for in the summer. Finally, after long years of drought, the summer monsoons swelled, the sky, I later wrote, *swept clean of cinder from our western fires.* All around me that moment: Chopin sonatas, what I had played as a girl on the piano, and what I had listened to my mother play, and the sleeping hummingbirds, and the sharpest quarter moon caught like a shining cloth in the windowpanes.

"Life is not people and scene, but thought and feeling," Stevens wrote. How I wanted to believe him that night, believe him now, when I look back into those windows as if the ineffable, and not the tangible, that flesh of snow, were all that mattered. *Light. Words. Fire to be lit come fall. Sound of wind. Always wind,* I wrote. *All I loved, here.* Yet, no matter what I wanted to believe, I knew that below me in the plains by morning the first funerals for the Aurora theatre massacre would begin, twelve dead, the largest massacre at that time in one shooting.

Skriniya, snow that never reaches the ground.

In 1904, at the height of the Colorado Labor Wars when the Western Federation of Miners fought with the Cripple Creek Mine Owners' Association over union power and demands for minimum safeguards within the mines, a man named Harry Orchard planted a bomb at the train depot in Independence, Colorado, a little ghost town I pass beneath the expanded Cripple Creek & Victor Gold, now Newmont, mine, killing fourteen men. Then in 1906, Orchard bombed the Vindicator Mine at Cripple Creek, killing another two men. And he dynamited a governor of Idaho without being physically present by rigging a gate with fishing line and explosives, a method of assassination new enough to law enforcement to buy Orchard a temporary alibi. Even at 9600 feet, it seems we cannot completely leave the fog of a frozen world behind.

Penstla is the Inuit word for the *idea of snow*. From the cabin, I watch the little snow given us take on the color of sky beneath noctilucent, *night shining*, clouds. The Utes, who traveled here so long ago to worship a god and the creation of a world, once bent saplings and tied them close to the earth with yucca rope. "Prayer Trees," they called them, these trees bowed to the ground and filling the wind, the Utes said, with prayer for eight hundred years.

I wonder if we look at the ugliness of the world that exists even here in this place I love, despite the mining district that surrounds it—the yellow spill of mine tailings I pass, the black maw of the mines beneath their gallows that some Utes may never have known—could we make a kind of beauty of it, dust like yellow roses brushed to the ground? Or a tree that never reaches the sky?

In another year, I wrote, in less than a year, a month, a week, a day, another Amish kindergartner in petticoats will be shot point-blank in the head at a chalkboard; another high school girl will text her parents, "I love you guys," then die at a mass murderer's hands.

Like Sisyphus, I wrote, *the endless boulder falling and us breaking apart. Again.*

How little I knew then. Of course later, I found out that King Sisyphus was no victim, but a sadist, a murderer for pleasure, a rapist, a con man who conned even the god of death when he bade his wife to throw his dead and naked body into the village square so that he might end up at the banks of the River Styx and thus deceive Persephone into allowing him to return to the upper world in order to chastise his wife for his "poor burial."

Stevens contends that the poet's purpose is to interpret the external world of thought and feeling through the imagination. I have lost count in these last years of atrocities since I wrote those words in my journal. And my beautiful Inuit words that made my mother on a darkest night exclaim with awe, that brought home to her and to me the husband and the father we were missing and, right there, on the edge of everything, our whole family still skating through the world on shining blades? These words were part of a ruse called the "Great Eskimo Vocabulary Hoax" by a British-American linguist and perpetuated by an entertainer in a satiric piece, *The Eskimos' One Hundred Words for Snow.*

Intla: snow that has drifted indoors. And not the glittering kind.

"Languages," experts say, "evolve to suit the ideas and needs that are most crucial to the lives of their speakers." How do I turn the ineffable into word? Be "spiritualized" before the time of a quickening spring that spreads lilac across computer-generated models, as if blooming lilacs were a blight? Or my little windflowers of purple, those pasque flowers called *Easter Flowers* that I seek out late or early spring in the last tatters of snow?

Four o'clock and the sun dives beneath the clouds. Shadows swamp the pastures and the old snows deepen to blue. I go outside to stand in the snow, to listen like the snow man who "nothing himself, beholds, /Nothing that is not there and the nothing that is," the wind I can hear drilling through the ghost aspen. Somewhere, I know, there are prayer trees double-downed in the snow, just as I know there is gold in the granite and the rose quartz the old homesteaders pick-axed into the glory holes I have so long stood at the glittering edge of.

Unearthing the 'Frail Children'

"ABSOLUTELY NOTHING HERE," Mother says.

She is my traveling companion beneath this broken volcano named Guffy along an ancient lakebed once rife with petrified sequoia stumps and post-dinosaur insects. The stumps, except for one, "Big Stump" that even the local Florissant officials of 1890 attempted to hack up and send to the Chicago World's Fair, have long been pilfered by visitors prior to the designation of the site as the Florissant Fossil Beds National Monument. And the seventeen hundred fossil species of leaf, bird, and insect once roiling the air above this vanished lake?

Long turned to stone.

In an article called, "Could Time End?" George Musser, a contributing editor for *Scientific American*, envisioned an "existential apocalypse" if time, as predicted by Einstein's relativity theory—from what I could make out—were to become extinct, to simply stop.

"No new life would emerge from ashes," Musser warns. No rebirth then, I try to explain to my mother, no molecular recycling in the same way there is none for these fossilized birds and insects caught by drifting volcanic ash some thirty-five million years ago, their sterile rebirths left only to man-made chisels and the geological hammers that release them, time for them in their own apocalypse both ending and everlasting. ("*I know that feeling,*" *Mother says.*)

As I write this, it is not my mother, tiny woman I now shepherd, nor her words, I am struck by, but a scar, skin, as I understand it now, its own fossil, its scars just above and below. The scar happened this way. I picked up an exacto knife to cut the plastic tag from a fake tiffany lamp I bought from a TJ Maxx clearance table. A tough plastic, so I swung the exacto knife down hard where I held the little ringlet away from the lamp's neck. The knife bounced, sliced through the flexor tendon that runs through the middle finger of my left hand near the joint at the tip. My finger wilted.

It was the first summer of our cabin far above this shimmering valley and the blue shadow of a pass where ancient Indians once carved their passages between worlds.

"Of course," Leonard said, as a trickle of blood wound down my hand. "Your mother's coming to visit."

Years later now, my mother lives seven minutes from me in a senior community home and we are driving through Teller County beyond the boundaries of a fossil monument to a little family-run quarry where I will try my hand at fossil-finding, wedging the rented razor blade between layers of paper shale, each skin of stone the remnant of a volcanic eruption, and then breaking apart old worlds sheath by sheath, peeling each apart to find their fossils—carbon shadow and mirror image lifting whole at my finger's touch if I am lucky and, if I am not, crumbling down to an altar of shale and pumice, memory and dream, where I kneel.

The skin's earliest scar is its most secret one, though common to all. But perhaps I am unfair to call it "scar"—that protuberance of vertebrae and embryonic tail bud, dimple of our tail bones that damns us to these fossilized remains I dig through, to fish and pig and to our *Catarrhini* brethren, ape and monkey. My own man-made scars spread out hungrily each passing year. The longest, the fine thin one made by my father when I was small, is a relic of the black mole he incised between my shoulder blades, what I sometimes glimpse in the mirror, my father's hands warm and steady there. And the tiny scar that once transformed landscapes for me, erupted the sandstone of ancient sea beds, of human sorrow, I was sure? Barely discernible, a prick of a green-balled pin at my finger's tip that once held my sutured tendon over the bone's joint, the pin pulled out by pliers long ago (*"No anesthesia. Hold your breath," the nurse practitioner said with a jerk*).

Each day after, I watched a ridge like a tectonic plate shifting millimeter by millimeter from the base of my nail upward, long after its wounding. In a cast for just one summer, that finger became a beacon, *Moby Dick*, I called it, of the maimed and the amputated—all of us of the mallet finger or the ghost finger or the peg-leg, the claw-hook or the widowed whose absences of limb or flesh I never noticed until my own scarring drew them.

"What happened?" these strangers kept asking me—and then an unconscious move on their part to hide the flesh they were missing or a short stillness in the fluttering of their scarred bodies revealed to me the landscape of the long bereft, time for them, too, (*as my mother would say she knows*), ending and everlasting.

Mother's call came at work, her voice muscular when she has news of death. "Your dad's dying. The nurses say it won't be long now."

I am buried in the open cubicle of the Internet startup I worked at before the community college with twenty somethings who stare at me and tap interoffice emails as I weep. I start to ask Mother, but how? He just moved from the state hospital to the nursing home with its Alzheimer's wing (*"That place of no return,"* Mother will tell me just this past week, *so many years later, "where everyone is hopeless"*). He just ran from the house we moved you to to the neighbor's garage. "'Begging for help,'" you said, "from me" (*"I've been kidnapped," you said he kept crying* out), you, this grieving woman he no longer could remember. But I don't ask and I don't say.

"You don't have to come," Mother said. "I just wanted you to know."

And hung up.

"You're just in the wrong pile," the kindly fossil quarry lady reassures me. Because I am apparently not a budding paleontologist, she brings me thick wedges of rock and enlists a ten-year-old named Ryan to show me how to tap my razor blade and butter knife with a chisel to slice my layers more precisely, to find bound within the brittle shale the ancient hieroglyphics I search for.

"A leaf," she tells me, pointing to the faintest elliptic shadow and its mid-vein track on the chip I hold, a microcosm of scar and fossil. "And this marks a root and this dark circle something decomposed before it could fossilize."

I show my mother this fossil—living matter trapped into paper shale, flesh and blood foreordained by ancient eruptions never to be recycled back into the earth. I think of Musser's existential apocalypse and of the arrow of time as we are said to perceive time—our perception of time always flowing from the known past to the unknown future—and of my father, the notion of being fossilized the closest I can get to understanding what the extinction of time might mean, and the extinction of a father.

I do not know what my mother is thinking.

Leonard meets with me with flowers. He never gives me flowers.

"You need to go," he says, Kitty and Mira hanging on his knees. "I'll stay."

I stand at that doorway even now, flowers, I want to say, *roses*, bending over my hands, the past flowing indiscriminately into present and more past. I remember calling my sister, arranging flights, calling my aunt to meet us at the airport and then calling my mother.

"Are you sure you want to come out?" she asks predictably, this woman I think I know who fears the sick and the dying, who avoids funerals, who never took us to a family funeral, refuses in writing to allow me and my siblings to one day have a funeral for her. ("*Burn me and just throw me out with the trash,*" she likes to joke with me.)

"End stage," Mother says to me over the phone. "You can tell by the breathing."

Socrates, repeating the words of a wise man, once said, "Our body is our tomb," the lives we lead now, Socrates wanted to reassure us, not our only ones, but one of many lives, our souls one day escaping these bodies that moor them to the earthly. In that ancient waterless lakebed called Lake Florissant, French for *flowering*, massive numbers of microscopic algae, a kind of diatom, once bloomed in tangent with volcanic eruptions even as other plants and animals died off, their stems and bodies drifting to the bottom of the lake. When whole colonies of diatoms died, they covered the volcanic ash that spewed for thousands of years and the organic material within it, entombing amidst global fires and shifting continental plates the fragile-winged and the wind-borne we find in this tiny quarry today, the little shadow lives I release with a butter knife.

I explain to my mother how I will preserve this single half-leaf as the fossil quarry lady has instructed me to with Elmer's glue and water. I will prop it on my bedside table, where sometimes half dreams of my father return (*I don't tell her this*) through the rods and cones of my shut eyes, this phantom light, this shadow of a father, not real but remembered, the arrow of time (*what keeps us*, I think, *from grieving forever over the unfixable past*), as Musser says, "A property not so much of time, but of the matter that occupies it."

My aunt and uncle greet us at the airport with offers of dinner before driving the hour to the nursing home that my mother put my father in after taking him out of the state hospital I last visited. (*Patient's gown, wheelchair with a tabletop, glasses sliding off his head, spittle of medication—trace fossils.*) "Bob, I have a surprise for you," Mother said then. "Look who is here." I held my hand out to him, momentary light crossing his face. He smiled, took my hand, kissed it, held it a moment too long.

"Watch out," Mother said as he bent my fingers back.

A dizzying sea of highway lights breaks around us now. My sister and I sit in the back seat of the aunt's car.

"Do you know what's going on?" she asks my aunt and the uncle who will drop dead in the kitchen of their Michigan cabin within scarcely a year. My sister is a nurse. "Why is he dying?"

No one knows.

Later, not this day nor that day, my mother will explain to me in a car amidst errands that she had to take him to the state hospital (*where my sister still questions the drugs they gave him*) because he was becoming violent. And my brother will give me these shadow images: our father the doctor (*what did he know even then that we did not*) begging my brother, "Get me out of here." He follows my brother to the automatic door as if he can go home—("*Did he really have Alzheimer's?*" *my sister will one day ask me over the phone.* "*It was the disease of that day.*")—my brother turning back to the closed door and the tiny window glass (*carbon shadow, mirror image*) our father presses his face against.

For a long time after his death, (*though Musser claims that the orderliness of matter in the universe gives us a sense of [progression] from past to future that doesn't actually exist*), my father returned to me in dreams, a flash in the scattered periphery, a wave, a half-smile. Once my brother and I climbed stairs with him, a small paper version of my father clinging to my brother's arms as I helped steer him up the stairs to where my mother sat against a wall, waiting. On the last step, my father stopped, leaned over, clear water rushing out of him, my mother crying out, and my father, the doctor, saying, *Well, that's it.* In the dream, I hold his arm again (*warmth of his skin, the weight and heft of it, scars that mark it*). Years later, in the new house my mother will want to move from because of her loneliness, (*especially at meals, she says*) I will remember that dream, sitting early, alone in my mother's kitchen, alone in her insurmountable quiet.

One of the student paleontologists bussed in from Louisiana hands the quarry lady a specimen he found on a pile of shale just ten feet from my mother and me. This is not the expected invertebrate fossil, but mirrors of a fish beautifully preserved, what we've all agreed by signed contract to hand over to the quarry lady and the Denver museum if we find one. The fish will be named for the student if it proves to be a new species, but the student will never be allowed to "own" it. All fossil lovers, except for my mother, we gather around the picnic table and give him our congratulations and condolences as the quarry lady wraps the fish for the museum.

I look around at my fellow excavators and wonder why do so many of us love fossils and their fixed pasts, the traces and casts of an underworld we so often walk oblivious upon, these beings, once souled or un-souled, compressed to carbon, molded in sediment, mineralized into stone, into time's end? When one of the sisters of this quarry unearthed a fossil wing and the long stalky leg of a bird, she closed the whole quarry down, gathered her family and sifted through the rubble until she could piece together the whole being compressed in its paper shale.

"Fossils underpin everything," a paleontologist interviewed by the *Smithsonian* explains. "If you want to look at how things came to be, you have to look at how it once was." History (*is it?*) is said to be made up of ages, one world ending to be replaced by another, reality and consciousness changing as crisis unfolds, as a father unfolds, as a mother unfolds. ("*I fell apart,*" *Mother tells Leonard,* "*one day alone at our favorite* restaurant. *I couldn't do it.*") In Greek, the word for age is *aeon*, a sphere of being emanating from the *godhead*, each new sphere more remote, more fastened to the material world the beleaguered soul must pass through in its search back for the divine. When Charlotte Hill, an 1800's Florissant homesteader turned fossil hunter, handed over the first Florissant fossils seen by paleontologists, she handed over the first fossil butterfly ever found in North America. So perfectly had the earth preserved this compression fossil that the "nervures," the veins of its wings, and the wings' color pattern made by scales only a single cell thick could be observed in the paper shale. (*This wing, one cell thick, like lightness remembered, like the soul's transparency preserved in rock and dream.*)

"Hurry," Mother said at the end of the long walk through the nursing home, my sister and I rushing through doorways we didn't know until our mother appeared against the linoleum. "I think he's been waiting for you. All day, we've been saying, '*Bob, just hold on, your girls are coming.*'"

A hospice nurse waves us through another doorway. My brother stands at the end of the bed where my father lies on his side panting, thinnest half-leaf I can imagine.

"Transitional breath," the hospice nurse says. "He's been doing it all day."

Mother leaves for a moment. My sister sits on the bed and takes his hand.

"Dad, it's okay. We're here, Dad. Let go, Dad. It's okay." This is what my sister sings. She strokes his hand, his shoulder. I sit on the bed below my father's curled knees and join in. His breathing changes. Slows. Breath. Breath.

We lean closer, counting the spaces between. The hospice nurse ushers my mother in. "Jean, it's time," she says. And then my father gasps, convulses up from the bed toward me, his face close to mine, his open mouth a black hole I stare into, and says something to me. Then falls back.

Samuel Hubbard Scudder, noted 19ᵗʰ century entomologist and insect paleontologist, called butterflies the "Frail Children of the Air" in a world "made up of eaters and eaten," and marveled at natural selection that imbued butterflies in the very last stages of their cyclical lives with the ability to mimic the world of beauty around them through their wings. "For the sole purpose of prolonging their aerial life," Scudder writes, "for the exceedingly few days of pairing and the deposition of eggs"—the intended insurance of a species for preservation.

Scudder said that of the fifteen thousand Florissant fossil specimens he touched, only eight were butterflies. Though he scoffed at the entomologists who believed that the root name for the butterfly came from the early Egyptians and their hieroglyphics that imbued the butterfly with the perfection of the soul—"All of which I in my ignorance," Scudder writes, "judge to be humbug"—Scudder named Charlotte Hill's butterfly *prodryas Persephone* for the mythic girl stolen from a field of flowers by a love-sick Hades in his golden chariot, Greek god of the underworld, that lost daughter for whom her grieving mother plummets the world and its time into winter and suffering.

One breath. We wait. Count. One breath. No breath.

"Bob," Mother says, touching him. The hospice nurse closes his eyes, his mouth. She leaves us to silence, to the coolness of his hands, his face, to time's arrow.

Then the living return: the hospice nurse and another nurse enter to check his vital signs, the time of his death, my mother asks for arrangements, for the nursing home car that will take him from the hospital, life whirling around him the way geese once circled him on a bench by a pond, that foreordained still center I could not touch.

Sometime, whether it was that day that my mother spoke while we waited for the hearse or another, she will ask me, "Do you remember when he sat up and leaned toward you?"

(*Yes*)

"You don't think he was trying to tell you anything, do you?"

(*Yes*)

"He wasn't."

How many years after does it take for my mother, now my traveling companion whose past life is so vivid to her as the present world fades, to answer my single question, to wedge her chisel into this fragile shale I have held since my father's death, "Why did he die?" (*Or perhaps did she? Earlier? And I simply wasn't ready to understand what I understand now?*) This is the heart of the story, isn't it? (*Kitty later scolding me for telling my sister this story over the phone on her birthday, my sister weeping*). Mother finally tells me what I suspected. "I remember walking into this big room filled with doctors and nurses," Mother says. "It was too much, his mother's and then my mother's. I couldn't, not again."

"We decided no feeding tube," she says, "so we moved him into the nursing home." The answer to all those questions over the years, here, now. "Why did he die so quickly?" people always asked. "Alzheimer's is a long disease." ("*Why do you have to tell anyone?*" *Kitty will ask me.* "*It's all in the past. What does it matter?*")

My mother, oblivious to me, chatters onto another story as we drive through the fossils of volcanic eruptions.

Musser, explaining time, even the most primal residue of time, says that "we have to have a sense of causality, that something we do has an effect in the world; and we have to have some kind of structuring to our existence." That is the reason for our perception of time as an arrow. I can tell you that I grew up with a loving mother and father on a farm in Ohio, a half country away on an ancient seabed of glacial fossils along the crest of a geological arch, fossils half a billion years old studding shale and limestone stowed in farm creeks and road slashes and the burying ground of my father and soon my mother's in the Murdoch cemetery. I knew nothing of this when I was child. All I knew was that I could walk down the field to the twelve yards of fenced creek my parents owned and pick up rocks scarred blue with fossil and hold in my hand brachiopods and cephalopods that live in our seas now or trilobites, sea travelers for 270 million years until time ended for them. When I told Mother these fossil facts once, she looked at me in disbelief, saying that in the eighty some years she lived in Ohio no one talked about fossils.

"Maybe that's it," she says. "Go to any creek and there were fossils. It wasn't such a big deal."

The summer my parents sold the farm, that year my father died, a new *aeon* I wasn't ready for, I drove those eleven hundred miles to pull that slab of sea rock from the creek and mortar it to the stone wall of our new cabin. Far above the sea floor now, my fossil rock sits opposite the mezuzah my husband inherited and nailed to the door frame, a scroll of paper prayer inside I can't forget that perhaps his aunts and father and mother, long dead too now, once finger-kissed as they passed through. This fossil rock, this mezuzah—the trace fossils of a moment, what the geologists call the "indirect evidence of a life" (*father I dream of, childhood mother I only half remember*).

I do feel the wonder of it—my mother walking through an old volcanic valley beside me, grumbling, but here, along the tracks of time and the bird and fish wedged in stone. But why the name *Persephone* for a lone butterfly fossil, one of Scudder's "frail children" left in that fossilized apocalyptic existence, the only one of its kind to rise from the stony underworld? Persephone, terrified and doomed to certain darkness, became instead the underworld's queen, rising as if reborn each spring to the light and flowers of her loving mother before returning to the world of the dead to guide those lost into their next lives ("*You know that's why I moved here,*" Mother says). I think of my father, frail child he became as his own mother became years before, both doomed to what we still think was Alzheimer's, this family darkness my brother and sister and I sometimes jest of in fear. And I think of my mother, frail child I tender now. ("*No mother should lose a child,*" Mother tells *me and tells me again her story of a friend's daughter dying of cancer, taken by her mother and family to a lake and to the trees she loved to die beneath. "In their arms," she says. "That's the way to do it.*") Named by the Greeks, *Theoi Khthonioi,* or *Chthonian gods,* Persephone as an underworld god "evokes," I read, "at once abundance and the grave," fitting descriptors for this quarry and the national monument where a whole other world I can barely grasp lies as frozen for eternity (*or for time's extinction*) as does my father. And my mother and me amidst the chipped fossils? Merely mortal.

Perhaps if we saw for ourselves the fragility of this butterfly compression fossil, we could better understood Aristotle's belief in spontaneous generation (*life out of non-life, butterfly out of rock*) rather than believe that the ferocity of this earth could somehow preserve the stone shadow of a butterfly the evolutionary biologists believe to have floated 90 million years ago past the heads of dinosaurs, those "terrible lizards," they were called, and the apocalyptic asteroid theorized to have turned in mass extinction these dinosaurs to fossil. But not the butterfly.

Florissant Fossil Beds Visitor Center informs us, and I point this out to Mother, *only one bone in a million is preserved as a fossil.* And yet, we have between us in the stone of my father preserved the most tender of wings, the most tender of souls (*carbon shadow, mirror image*).

Kitty, when she first interned at the environmental center that summer in Aspen, asked how she could warn visitors of the potential dire effects of climate change without sounding too harsh. Ask them, I told her, if they want humans to become just fossils, as if, I realize now, that this fate was the worst that could happen. But I wonder. An attorney for The Defenders of Florissant in the 1960s arguing against land developers called this vast expanse of hidden fossils a "34 million-year-old record, a record you might say written by the mighty hand of God." There is something beautiful in this endeavor, this fossil-finding, despite my mother's determined belief that there is absolutely nothing here, (*holiness for my mother always something never to speak, better to chitchat*). The fossil of a butterfly forever echoes the beauty of an extinct world while even the most clueless of tourists with their cardboard boxes, bleary magnifying glasses, and rusted chisels make "eureka" discoveries amid the common leaf ghosts and the scattered seed pollen from which a flower or a sequoia turned to stone once bloomed.

Stephen Hawking, in *The (Elusive) Theory of Everything*, says that in "quantum physics, the past, like the future, is indefinite and exists only as a spectrum of possibilities." Some thirty-five million years ago, a half leaf fell amid the blasts of a volcano and its rain of ash. And so did a butterfly. Tectonic plates shifted. Glaciers heaved. Whole species perished. Men and women wrapped their frail dead in the cloths of mummies like chrysalis and thought them immortal, while a girl who never existed still walks each spring through flowered fields and listens to the dead calling her back and to the mother who needs her. Who could have planned for the stone shadow of this half leaf I hold in my hands and the worlds it unburies? Or the stone veins of a butterfly wing, lighter than even the air we still breathe or the soul that one day will escape or the ghost fathers we still dream of? Or the mothers, half-seeing and fearful, who search out their lost daughters so their daughters can shepherd them through the same ancient blue passages and shimmering valleys they once feared to lead their husbands through?

My ten-dollar hour over, we follow Ryan, my trusty ten-year-old guide, to the tool shed where he sells the rocks and fossils he collects from the quarry. I watch Ryan wander through his wares and remember the bloody-toothed shell I once found on the farm and kept in my box for the cast-off, a fossilized snail encased in the mouth of it, a doe-eyed crater of infinite light and black hole I still yearn for, a fossil long stolen I hope by someone lost or bereft who fingered it helplessly, perhaps, at some poetry workshop I gave, then vanished, leaving me with only quick verses or dreams of how a calf's eye looks half closed when it sucks your finger for milk on a father's and a mother's farm you left so long ago and love, still.

Trace fossils, dear Mother (*time not extinct, but indefinite*).

GRAVITATIONAL WAVES AND THE
CANIS LUPUS

Awe resembles the bird that makes you quiet
—Rumi

LEONARD STUDIES THE COSMOS these days, and so I do, too. He settles into a family room chair in our suburban Littleton house, resting the "good" knee he injured only months after retirement from his community college by doing sit ups in the basement. He watches video lectures on string theory and Einstein's *Theory of Relativity*, his computer screen filled with phantasmal black holes and black matter amid the rainbow blaze of galactic gases and galaxies. NASA emails me *SpotTheStation* now. They tell me when the International Space Station, ISS, will orbit over Victor and Cripple Creek 250 miles over my head, pinpointing for me the space station's exact appearances and disappearances, always from the westerly to the easterly sky, the youngest unblinking "star" of my cosmos disappearing with a magician's "poof" into the Puebloan sky glow.

Einstein said that "the most beautiful thing we can experience is the mysterious." I don't know why I find the emails that NASA sends me so fascinating in contrast to the whole multi-dimensional universe Leonard balances on his lap with a tea cup, especially since it took me until my more than middle age years to google a listserve and sign up with a single zip code to find the brightest light, NASA tells me, (man-made as the space station is), within the billion-year haze of a galaxy I have wished upon since I was a child naming stars by my mother's farm pond.

Tonight, the space station will ride the sky eighty-eight degrees above the Cripple Creek horizon at 6:45 p.m. and appear from the northwest for exactly three minutes in the air at almost nine fist lengths—I've calculated this before—above the ground. It will then skim the cusp of Nipple Mountain before passing into the southeastern sky at 15,500 miles per hour.

Lost straw, ember, silvery river, cow's milk, pathway of birds—these make up the litany of names our most ancient ancestors gave our Milky Way, where now a space station I am always searching for orbits the earth sixteen times a day, a tiny manmade moon lit beyond the earth's visible shadow. But I will miss it this time, NASA's email, as always, dinging my Outlook when I am hours away in these suburbs, buried by a dome of neighborhood light.

Psychologists have a term, *hedonic adaptation*, for when we lose our sense of "awe," whether for nature or the man-made, a word derived from an Old Norse word, *agi*, that means awe as in "wonder at the sublime" and "terror," and the Greek word *achos*, or "pain," perhaps the root of Achilles' name, that half-celestial hero his sea nymph mother, frightened of the fate the prophecies foretold, dipped by a heel into the River Styx and rendered, almost, invulnerable.

"I'll never get better," Leonard says, words he worries like rosary beads since tearing his meniscus in the basement and "testing" it for months until even the Kaiser doctor, once so sunnily optimistic, said, "Surgery." *Hedonic adaptation* is the "the psychological process by which humans adapt to negative or positive stimuli over time." It's why the paired bluebirds, I tell Leonard, nesting on the corner of the cabin porch beam that we always greet with such joy each spring may one day seem a nuisance, chittering at their fledglings and keeping us, their household interlopers, from our rocking chairs. Or why, after the first few times we awake in the dark to the wild din of coyotes—Navajo's barking dog, trickster dog—that migrate our suburban water ditches, and rise, heart pounding, to peer

94

together through our windows into the unfathomable, we might one night merely shove the window shut and sleep.

But Leonard cannot unworry himself.

For me, each time I pass the threshold of our cabin door between the gold fire of our wood stove and the crystalline dark sky only a portion of our human world can see and I find myself shivering outside alone in the din of night howls from the neighbor's hybrid wolves—"If you ever see them outside our fence, be careful," Larry and Tami, Ohio transplants, too, warn me—I still stand full-faced to the sky in awe. Here, right now, a space ship made of aluminum and glass sparks into being the minute NASA tells me it will and it migrates through the same scattered Milky Way that lights Leonard's face from a computer screen in our family room, my hobbled husband, who, for seven months now, has orbited a dimension I don't quite understand.

"You know," Mother keeps reminding me, the same mother who keeps asking me why she isn't dead yet (*As soon as I find a big knife, I'm going to cut my throat*, she jokes today), "Leonard's really depressed."

This fall, our valley neighbor who grew up on a Nebraskan ranch, tells me in passing that "coywolves" roam our parceled land in packs of six and eight, coywolves, those large muscled hybrids first bred by the co-mingling of coyote and northwestern gray wolf.

"That's too big of a pack. I'll shoot first, then I'll think," she says of this Darwinian phenomenon she would kill. I warn Leonard, lost in his static pixel stars again, of the coywolves and our armed neighbors, though I am the one to wander our land alone, not him.

"What is wrong with people?" he asks, my city boy peering at me over his computer screen, an ice pack jimmied to his knee.

In her poem, *The Moose*, Elizabeth Bishop describes riding on a bus through the night, listening to an "old conversation—/

not concerning us...but recognizable, somewhere" until suddenly "a moose came out of the impenetrable wood...high as a church."

"Why, why," she asks us, "do we feel/ (we all feel) this sweet/ sensation of joy?" until all that is left of that moment is "a dim/ smell of moose, an acrid/ smell of gasoline," the moose fading from awe into the familiar. Years ago, Leonard and I walked a summer-thick trail past the Maroon Bells, every seeable space doused by leaf and blossom, my thirty some year husband quiet ahead of me until a quick explosion of sound I thought his stopped us.

"Are you all right?" I started to ask and then saw through the screen of brush a pair of moose grazing from within the creek, *only an arm's length away*, I thought and pulled Leonard close to me, familiar sweat and heat beneath my hand until we fled.

I ask Leonard about the most recent phenomena in astronomy that he's been talking about for months. He looks up from his seat by the gas fire in the family room. "You know," I say. "When all the scientists aimed their telescopes at the stars?"

"The collision of two neutron stars," he says. "Dead stars." He rustles his science magazine at me and continues reading. I borrow his computer and click around until I find a page of astronomy links, each with a superlative title using words like *First Ever* and *Dawn of an Era*. *Kilonova*: an explosion of light and gravitational waves (*What are they*? Leonard tests me. *Like a pond, time and space rippling?* I hazard) caused by two stars colliding, this one, the first to be observed happening in a galaxy just 130 million light years away from us, exploding back in time with the dinosaurs and the first flower bloom.

Leonard watches me. "Einstein's relativity theory predicted these gravitational waves erupting from black holes he didn't even believe in." Einstein is one of Leonard's heroes. "He went to the hospital, his heart failed, and they burned him, you know," Leonard tells me for the third or fourth time. I find artists' renderings showing multicolored collisions of neutron stars born billions of light years ago and caches of gold and plutonium the explosion was said to create. I find an actual image of the explosion, aftermath of these neutron stars' death spiral, taken from the Hubble telescope—a pinprick of light barely discernible at the edge of a black blob.

"Unbelievable," Leonard says.

"Does the station appear and then disappear because of the light of the moon?" FAQ at *Spot The Station* asks, as if this man-made marvel were folkloric, ruled by the whimsy of wind and fire, light and darkness. "Does the wolf howl at the moon?" my wide-eyed daughters would ask during bedtime storytelling, wolf the mythic creature of both Aesop's *Fables* and Isaiah's biblical verse, this blessed wolf grazing with the lamb on the Lord's holy mountain as if it, too, had been held by a heel, dipped into water and made almost immortal.

A few years ago, Lydia Millet, in a *New York Times* op-ed, "High Noon for the Gray Wolf," lamented over a bill designed to delist the gray wolf from federal protection. The federal government had already once stripped Wyoming of its jurisdiction over the wolves because of its "kill-on-sight approach to wolf management" and the 3,500 wolves killed by ranchers and zealot "wolf killers" that were caught in a "blood lust," as the op-ed described it, holdovers from the bounty slaughter of gray wolves in the first half of the 20th century which caused their decimation from millions to mere hundreds.

What struck me most in the editorial, besides the atrocities aimed at the gray wolf, was Millet's understanding of our need for awe, for the mysterious, no matter how fleeting or frail. Millet lamented over the possibility of her daughter never experiencing the sudden sighting of a wolf, emissary, like Bishop's moose, of "a world where something beautiful and wild lurks at the edge of sight."

Some years ago, I took our Joey to the woods to teach him to follow me, this mutt puppy we adopted the year Kitty and Mira left for college, wrapping his front legs around my ankles when he tired. I looked up and saw against the snow, larger than I had ever imagined in the nocturnal din of cabin circlings, a coyote or wolf, I did not know which then, a body's length away. I remember not fearing it, thinking how surprisingly clean it was, its neck a white ruff of winter fur, and how it had simply appeared as if shimmering out of the trees to greet us, out of the very air, this coyote or coywolf or phantasmal wolf motionless, measuring us, until I swept Joey into my arms and it vanished, soundless as a human star.

I ask Leonard, buried in his computer, a heart monitor now attached to his chest because of the strange flickerings of his heart he has sensed since knee surgery when he flatlined (*nothing to worry about*, the doctors said), "What has happened? Where is the awe?"

"I am always looking at the universe," Leonard reminds me, peering over his reading glasses.

"*We're* always looking at the universe," I remind him.

When the gray wolf was introduced into Yellowstone, it caught the imagination of the public, igniting what Arthur Middleton in the *New York Times* described as having been "a flagging American interest in wildlife and ecosystem conservation." Have they really become so familiar, such nuisances to us now, these wolves once hardy enough to survive a Pleistocene Ice Age and the large-scale extinction of mastodons, of saber-toothed cats, of giant ground sloths, and teratorn birds with wing spans twenty-five feet wide? On a community discussion board, I find those, who support the newest "War on Wolves" congressional bill, name-calling the advocates of wolf preservation they argue with "ignorant wolftards" because they object to the killing of wolves and their pups in their dens, by "any means," a provision I am reluctant to follow up on for the details.

Even Mother quips, "Well, why don't we just shoot 'em?" when I take her to visit the Colorado Wolf and Wildlife Center in Divide. I explain to her how this facility cares for wolves and hybrids that cannot live in the wilds of the lower 48 states, even despite so much public enthusiasm for the specter of dispersal wolves migrating out of the invisible borders of Yellowstone that the Colorado Wildlife Commission adopted a contingency plan for the wolves imminent and, as they said, "welcomed" return.

Mother laughs. "Don't write down what I just said. Who knows what people will think of me." But I do.

Sometimes when Leonard and I carry his homemade telescope, with the professionally polished mirror Leonard babies—*too much dust and wind tonight*, he'll say—and the sun slants down toward the Arkansas valley below us, I can make out the roof lines of an abandoned outbuilding where a woman is said to have once raised the wolves she found here (*real ones*, neighbors claim) amid the crags. But I wonder.

The last Colorado wolves were killed in the 1940s. Since then, wolf spottings have been rare and those spottings of dead wolves—a wolf struck dead by a motor vehicle on Highway 70 near Idaho Springs and a collared wolf poisoned in Eagle County by a compound banned in Colorado since 1972. The most recent wolf spotting was that of a wolf shot and killed near Wolford Mountain Reservoir by a hunter mistaking the wolf for a coyote. Despite the coyote in the woods I once imagined to be a wolf or coywolf I like to think of as wild, I have never seen a wolf outside of the centers that protect them. When Kitty and Mira were young, I took them to a center near Westcliffe and we watched the mostly hybrid wolves eat donated road kill, just one wolf, "pure," they said, which, as part of an educational program, was allowed to lick in greeting the teeth of the visitors who sat in circles around it. I think of Bishop who glimpsed a moose on a "moonlit macadam" and found it as "otherworldly" as I did this wolf in that moment, raising its head skyward and keening, the moon and all its orbiting companions earth-shadowed, until, finally, the other rescued and relocated and hybrid wolves inside their wire pens howled, spun the air wild.

Sometime soon, Leonard's knee will heal and his heart, too, I hope. Then we will once more carry his telescope out into the night so that he can adjust numerical markings and star coordinates and swing us back home, to our home, through whirlpool galaxies and globular clusters and the mysterious gravitational waves, which can shake a universe and a man. And northwest of us, the sky painted a dull sheen from the gold mine lights and the far house of a millionaire no one ever sees, perhaps a single light, a pin prick, will float over us in the din of coyote and hybrid wolf, Leonard's familiar shadow still there, amid the galactic shine, long after I sleep.

SLOW ARROW

I AM THINKING ABOUT MUSHROOMS because my sister, head tilted at her godless sister, has asked me if I always write of death. And because my new neighbors, in the draw just below our broken fence line, have scraped what I thought was Eightmile Creek into a dam, a fishing hole they always "dreamed of."

The end of summer here and I want to write of summer, how flowers remind us of what has risen: the delicate breath of those we loved gone under, a tendril of green we want to touch—a bent petal, a circlet of seed.

But here is the mushroom.

The first time I think I truly saw mushrooms was in Mary Oliver's poem of the same name. She balanced them "in the earth on one hoof," made them "skulls," transformed them into "flocks of glitterers," then vanquished them beneath "shining fields of rain."

I think I have always been half-afraid of mushrooms, their abruptness of being after days of dampness, their bloodless pallor—a kin of clay in a litter of leaves—molded out of the rot and dankness just beneath the hinged door of our earth. If flowers are the poet's beloved "airy soul" crept back, then the mushroom is the fleshy body in wait beneath a river of moles and feeding cicadas. Both are equally part of this world.

And what of my new neighbors?

They began the first year of their suburban exodus onto our mountain plain by leaving the bloody carcass of an elk outside their modular cabin. When the poet Wordsworth, purveyor of beauty, speaks of beauty, when his "heart with pleasure fills," it fills with the daffodil, not the mushroom. And, certainly, not the hulk of an elk birthing blowflies.

Yet, my neighbors with their trophy camera wired to a tree outside their cabin door and their wild hopes of marauding bear and mountain lion drawn close to its shutter distance, despite their tiny cabin balanced on its precarious concrete blocks, are as equally a part of this place as is the yellow wildflower I pick for the glass vase on my dining table and the mushroom that spreads its spores at my feet.

When my sister asks me why I write of death in a world filled with the natural beauty she takes comfort in—those sparkling lakes, turquoise skies, and "colorful flowers" that my students fill their essays and poems with—I am helpless to answer. It's what the literary writer does, I should tell her; it's the way to get beyond what journals like *Ecotone or Flyaway* call "the hushed tones and clichés of much of so-called nature writing," or the "simply lovely meandering poetry about the beauty of a field of wheat or a sunset."

But what is beauty in nature, especially when the human, when the neighbor, interrupts the wild? I often ask my community college students not to write about the everyday beauty of nature, what they have grown up hearing about, but about the beauty that is harder to see—like the calf I have tried to write about for years now, the one I found dead one spring below the cabin. *Half angel shell*, I wrote, *now sea sound*, all winter the predators sculling his collapsing belly, cleaning out his soft organs *in the craterous dark, in the eye socket dark.*

In her essay, "An argument about beauty," Susan Sontag argues that "the most stirring beauty is the most evanescent …it reminds us of nature as such—of what lies beyond the human and the made." To understand the complexity of earth, to express beauty in all its unfathomableness even as it passes from us, is what I know I want, the things of this earth we have loved and lost cycling into transcendence.

But still, I look through my journal for moments to give my sister that she might love—*boughs of descended rain, gauze of air.* And then I find the miller moth that once circled the light bulb of my reading lamp, the crush of its wings against the hot glass, how I wrote of catching it in mid-air, the tiny ragged thread of its life less than breath against my palms until I released it, by morning its frailty littering the floor.

In spring, we smelled death, I want to write, despite my sister's admonishment, a gritty tendril of it cast through the air, the dogs mysteriously oblivious to it. But Leonard and I stayed, anxious at the scent of it, until we found it: a fawn against the rocks, its neck broken, splayed back, its ribs like a fan unfolded. A fresh kill, most likely mountain lion, someone told us later, berating us for going back at evening, and then the next morning, too— the mountain lion surely treed nearby—to find what was left of the fawn: a leg, hair, the rack of its tender spine.

Death, but a terrible beauty, too. Yes, I want to say to my sister, we were tossed from your paradise, but to what more beautiful place than earth with not just its minions of fish and bird calling out to be named, but its scoured bones and yellow leaves we call "trembling" so soon to vanish against the blue blaze of a noon—as is the turkey vulture that soars above a fallen fawn?

"Exactly how many," interrupts Mother, my cabin companion once more and unappreciative transplant from the red autumns of Ohio, "yellow leaves can you look at?"—my reveries ended.

The Caterpillar stuck in the creek early in the summer. I saw it from the once solitary ridge I share with my new neighbors, and where now a large metal canister hangs from a tree, a kind of "elk-baiter." It disperses, my neighbors explain, alfalfa pellets to draw elk to the second wildlife camera they've secured to another tree nearby and what, in fall, I fear, will lure the elk to the sighting scopes of their rifles.

"Better wear orange," Sally, my valley neighbor warns me again, her husband, Scott, a conscientious hunter who is known to douse himself with estrous doe urine before bow-hunting.

When the bulldozer stuck, the creek pushed hard around it, half-swallowed it despite the bunker of mud that Dave, the cattle rancher who trades scraping our two-wheel lane for cattle grazing rights, scraped up from the creek bed for the dam. "Well," Dave told me later, "we'll just take it apart piece by piece," and he described to me how the chain rigged to their truck to free it snapped, bursting through the back window, his wife Tandy almost smashed in the head, death, it seems, my dear sister, everywhere.

But I am thinking about ancient water rights now, not death nor beauty. And of the man, my new neighbor, who owns one slim finger of land across a wide valley and will go against a whole history of community to dam a creek: the *acequias* trenched by hand by our early Spaniards and the placer claims of 1800s gold miners who created still current "first in time, first in right" water doctrines. I have known a certain Colorado water lawyer for about three decades now and given his comments on the water rights of those who have first claim on water, I'm pretty sure that it is neither legal nor community-minded to plug up an entire creek in our watershed with a bulldozer.

"I can't believe it," Mother says, in her red coat, her walking stick in hand as we trudge up the lane with the dogs to see some more yellow leaves. I describe to her this small valley waterway below us, this nameless creek just a blue squiggle mapped out in the Beaver Creek watershed, where Kitty and

Mira once waded amid tiny fish and bright snakes. Once it was strong enough to knock down the broken stone bridges that still crisscross it, built by other inhabitants long dead. John Wesley Powell, the 19th century explorer of the American West, said that within the watershed, a natural conduit of precipitation, "All things are inextricably linked." And now this creek—that has braided the floor of this valley, carved banks and deep tunnels beneath fallen logs and boulders, watered elk, deer, birds, bear, bobcat, aspen, conifer and the wildflowers and the mushrooms of every summer for as long as anyone here can remember— plugged, for a fishing hole.

I remember walking down the draw through the aspen shoot, a faded cow path wandering the hillside to the valley and passing the small detritus of neighbors, here and gone: rusted farm machinery, abandoned spring cellars, holes dug for gold, and the fencing wires still nailed to trees to keep cattle in. It seems we leave and yet our detritus lives on, even as nature slowly takes over in its fierce and beautiful regularity. How I hated it when these new neighbors first camped below our property, an American flag sticking out between the concrete blocks they stacked for the cabin to come. The meadow, once small and beautiful with only a broken-down hunter's shack and towering aspen trees to ring it, was strewn with campers and outhouse tents.

But then I saw the homemade "footer" the couple had poured for the cabin they dreamed of. How each had so carefully put their hand prints into the concrete, a small child's there, too, and then the paw prints of a dog, each name written out in such joy below, each name—forgive me, my sister—*writ in water*, I think, words the poet Keats asked to be engraved on his tombstone.

The new neighbors have wired another wildlife camera to a tree down by the creek and their dam. "A hundred pictures," they told me it took, "ninety-eight percent triggered by cows."

I take Leonard to the ledge to show him the dam, my mother waiting for us in a lane of yellow leaves like the final one that will one day take her places I still know nothing of, despite my mother's belief that I am the right one to guide her. How do we reconcile faith here, beauty or death, or a mother's death? I remember how I could barely stand to look at the calf, but I did anyway, season after season, as if decay alone propelled transcendence, wishing, as I did, for my sister's sweetness. *Note the black shadow,* I wrote, the oil staining its perimeter, how the bones kept scattering, as if swept by some invisible tide. Is this what the calf falters into earth for, I wondered, bloats skyward cell for cell: *puma at hushed dark, the coyote's tongue, and the bulbous may flower, so tissue-thin?*

Leonard stops to rest his healing knee at the top of the ridge beneath a pine tree, and I go down alone to stand on the stones to wait for him, to finger-trace an empty creek bed to a dam I can only curse. Whole trees, the off shoots of an aspen colony, a thick comb of them, have long grown over where the body of the calf once lay and I have learned to search for mushrooms, to say their names: *Shaggy Mane, Grisette, Hawks Wing.* Sometimes, they billow out of the earth as big as skulls, *Tête de mort,* we call them, filled with trillions of dark spores that I could circle this whole earth with. And some mornings, clouds push up from the Arkansas Valley, whole horizons disappearing, the world I can see a mere fifty yards wide.

But, sometimes, beauty without warning does come—here, a mushroom or, even, a calf, or a mother in a red coat blazing against the gold. Or a herd of elk you never expected sunk to their bellies in a quiet fishing hole your neighbor always dreamed of.

Our breath, I write my sister, *flies from us like small sparrows.*

SKYGLOW

n/a

SOMETIMES, LEONARD WAKES ME at two in the morning to watch the gibbous moon swallowed by Grouse Mountain. On winter nights, moonrise starts left of the butcher's abandoned camper trailer where once this retired neighbor, vanished now, wiggled his ten blocky fingers at me and said, "Thirty years, and not a one lost," his wife rolling her eyes beside him.

Leonard and I, too, are only temporary here, sporadic suburban migrants who will drive hours past slow rivers of fly fishermen, their fly lines like gossamer against the rocks, and then climb the deep shadows of Rainbow Pass to alight for a few days near the rim of this small canyon someone long ago named *Phantom*, that Indian princess, *Dark Flower*, it's said, still heard weeping—if we would only listen—for her dead betrothed.

According to *The Bortle Dark-Sky Scale*, a chart created to quantify the effect of light pollution on the "observability" of celestial objects, the darkest sky measured at *zenith*, the most direct point over our heads, is ranked Class 1.

"Theoretical," the editors at *Sky & Telescope* call this sky. "An observer's Nirvana."

It seems that even at 9600 feet altitude, even if our atmosphere were not a morass of human-made *spill light* and *light trespass*, the earth itself lights the visible sky with *airglow*, "planetary emissions." Electrons lost in the ultraviolet of daylight recombine at night with oxygen and nitrogen atoms to create a green *lambent halo* from equator to pole, a halo so beautiful that one of the space station astronauts tweeted it to those of us in the unseeing world below.

To hope to see the faint and the far-flung celestial objects in the night sky, one must learn the art of dark-adaptation, to quicken the sensitivity of the eye to the dim starlight that exists within this partial darkness. To hasten dark-adaptation, you must use what's called "averted vision," and look askance at the object so that its light hits the most sensitive area of the eye and, thus, becomes visible. The risk, though, is that the light might hit the "blind spot" where the optic nerve exits the eyeball, and then, as if you were blind, nothing of the object will be seen.

Finally, light shuts, the last of it caught in the long flat clouds at sunset that Mother calls "weird," but now, one year after moving to Denver, and years after my father's death, adds the word, "beautiful."

"I've never seen that before," she tells me. "All that gold light held in the clouds."

My mother watches the sky from a ninth-floor apartment in the middle of this town turned bedroom community to Denver. At night the lighted townscape I sometimes watch with her is a tatting of shielded luminaires and pole mountings, a river of headlights, and an orange sky glow of illuminated baseball parks.

The eastern sky from my mother's window is a Class 7 on the Bortle Scale, *Suburban/urban transition*, where the whole background of the night sky is a dim white, the Milky Way— that collective star glow that Leonard and I gaze at in the thin air above our mountain cabin—nearly invisible. The hundred and ten deep sky objects a French astronomer named Messier recorded back in the 1800s with the equivalent of a child's toy telescope today have vanished from our sight. "Pale ghosts" is how *Sky & Telescope* describes what is left to see in this Class 7: diffuse nebular, globular and galactic clusters of stars nicknamed *Andromeda*, *Butterfly*, the *Seven Sisters*, and the *Beehive Cluster*, its starlight four hundred million years old and traveling five hundred and seventy-seven years to reach us, only to be dimmed by our excess light.

Science also tells me that I can see 19 quadrillion miles (that's fifteen zeroes tacked on after the 19) or a little more than 3200 light years away. My mother peers out her window when I tell her this and half-jokingly says that this is not quite what she can see. Low-pressure glaucoma. Macular degeneration.

More and more, Mother holds my arm, whether noon or dusk.

This is the real dark, I always want to think, these forty acres at night beneath our cabin balcony and its tiny shred of nightlight. The earth is an inky pitch here, unfathomable beneath this firmament I keep forgetting in the suburbs with my mother, *skyglow* and *uplight* dissembling the very stars our ancients once named into now truant gods.

I am still trying to understand what a star is. I ask Leonard what constellation in early winter will be most visible at the cabin. Twenty-three hundred years ago, Aristotle believed all "heavenly bodies" floating above our planet were perfect and everlasting, even the asteroids of our solar system that we know now as "shattered worlds," imperfect fragments of the long vanished. Homer named Venus, our wandering star, both "Phospheros" and "Hesperos," never knowing his morning and evening stars were the same. Phospheros was the "dawn-bringer," while Hesperos was named after the stargazer who nightly climbed Mount Atlas only to be carried off by wind to burn forever as the ancient Greek's "fairest star" in the heavens. *Burnham's Celestial Handbook*, an observer's guide that Leonard studied when he first took out his six foot long telescope beneath the stars, is an old book now from its 1979 copyright, but it tells me still of the things I cannot see nor understand, of light years and radiant energy, of star clusters and dark gases, super giants and red dwarf stars, and of the supernova, the complete destruction of a giant star, its luminosity equaling that of all the other billions of galactic stars out there. Somehow, despite Jung's admonishment that our sole purpose is to kindle meaning, this comforts me, this light in the dark that we cannot see.

"Orion," Leonard tells me, the constellation in our southwestern skies marked by three stars, the belt of Orion, that mythical hunter and celestial warrior of ancient Greece, lover of a king's daughter, I find out, who was struck blind by the king until the gods took pity on Orion and sent him to stand before the rising sun, his sight returned, everything I thought random not, I am now realizing, but connected to my mother. Before the Greeks, the early Egyptians believed Orion to be the reincarnation of Osiris, god of the underworld, who gave the dead passage: *With Orion you shall descend, The Pyramid Texts* of the 5th Dynasty say, *into the western region of the sky.* Here Sothis, goddess of Sirius the dog-star, guided the pharaohs on what the Egyptians called *the goodly roads . . . in the sky in the Field of Rushes* so that those dead could become what they thought were "imperishable" stars.

I think of my father, long dead, waiting for my mother in that small midwestern Murdoch cemetery I wandered through as a child and when I was a young girl waiting for love, honeysuckle pinned to the fence line between our farm and the toppled gravestones, and of the ashes one day I will gently carry there.

"I don't care," Mother says, when I tell her what I want to do. "I'll be gone."

Of the 400 billion stars they say exist in the Milky Way, our galaxy thick with dark matter and the dust of the cosmos, I realize I can see not even a fraction.

And of my mother? Even less.

"Well, I'm here," Mother said at the airport that day she arrived, without bag or carry-on, almost walking past me where other plane travelers disembarked the escalators into the arms of their loved ones until I reached out and touched her. When she arrived from her beloved Ohio, my father left behind in that bee-sung cemetery, she was not the woman I quite remembered, her bones either compressed by gravity or broken down by the osteoporosis that is the fate of women in our family.

"I hope I stroke out before I go blind," she tells my siblings and me.

"I'm trying to remember that poem by Keats," I say to Mother. She has been here almost a year and I sit companionably with her by her apartment window. "The one about that star—."

Mother gets up from her chair before I am even done talking, pulls out a hard-bound book in a worn case from her mini bookcase, finds a page already bookmarked, and hands the book to me. *Bright Star,* by John Keats. Next to the poem is a little penciled-in notation in my mother's handwriting: *for Fanny Brawne,* the woman Keats loved and could not marry. The book? A *Little Treasury of Poetry.*

"My mother gave this to me when I was twenty-one. She knew I liked to read poetry," Mother says.

I look at my mother. For over fifty years, I have written and studied poetry and she has never once shared this book nor her interest in poetry. Once I asked her about a personal journal of hers I had stumbled on and if she had written others.

"Oh, I had journals," she tells me. "Lots. But that's another life, another time."

She jabs her thumb over her shoulder and chuckles.

"All gone."

I lean my head back over the balcony railing to watch the moonless sky. *Tramp stars,* the early Greeks called the wandering planets. The Babylonians read omens in the stars, believed for so long to be "flawless and eternal." Minute by minute, the constellations that these early astronomers watched, too, drift westward while those fragments of "shattered worlds" pass by us toward infinite space. I keep thinking of Keats, stargazer as my husband and I are, dying in a transient world, who wrote of *Polaris*, fixed, it seemed then, at the celestial North Pole, and of his "fair love's ripening breast":

> *Awake for ever in a sweet unrest*
> *Still, still to hear her tender-taken breath,*
> *And so live ever—or else swoon to death.*

Keats believed that "What the imagination seizes as Beauty must be truth—whether it existed before or not." Billions of meteorites, fine as sand, spark against our air and, if I look long enough, I can track the unwavering pinheads of satellites and space stations beneath the stars. I ask myself what Keats would say now of this "celestial clutter": thousands of satellites orbiting the earth at 17,000 miles an hour or of the cast-off nuts and bolts and the one lost glove of an astronaut or the uncountable paint flecks and the plastic shards said to circle us in Low-Earth orbit. But then I remember that he believed it was the poet's quest to find beauty in a world doomed to suffering and death.

"I am certain," Keats wrote to his friend, Benjamin Bailey, "of nothing but of the holiness of the Heart's affection."

Past midnight, the moon will again circle over Nipple Mountain where an ancient hibernating bear will rouse itself in spring into the cross hairs of a spotting scope owned by Dave, our leaser of fields, who has trained his telescope on this lair for so many years to watch this slow awakening. *Mythic*, we call it now. Then, finally, the moon will descend to moonset, so slowly it seems—our eyes heavy with sleep, Leonard's body and mine trembling together against the jagged, frosted air—until the mountain snags it and we watch a moon so beautiful that even my mother can see it plummet past the visible edge.

I try not to seem too greedy now and leaf nonchalantly through the little slips of paper my mother has folded up and tucked into the front cover of her *Little Treasury of Poetry* book: a poem written by my grandmother to my mother on her 21st birthday, poems on loneliness, one by an ancient Chinese poet, and a French love poem, translated by my father, two years before he married my mother, with a little postscript he wrote at the end: *P.S. French.*

On the back of the poem, my mother typed in the English translation, so long ago that I can barely make out the letters where the page folds.

"Well," Mother says, "your father was barely passing French, so I had to do something."

Mother and I laugh.

Amour, my father signed.

Twelve times the moon has orbited the earth since my mother moved here, or thirteen, if the blue moon—the "betrayer moon"—rose even once, that bitter Lenten moon of repentance, of reflection I had once forgotten. I think of my mother at her city window, this tiny widow, who once carried me, waiting to be lead through the darkness, and of Sothis, guide I had never heard of, goddess of Sirius, of the brightest star I can see beneath Orion, guiding the dead to an afterworld I once knew nothing of, its stars, once thought imperishable, faded and shattered, but still beautiful.

To our eyes that must dark-adapt, the moon is amorphous stone the sun lights into *scythe* and *disk*, this earthly world in the moon's marble-cast etiolated except when sometimes *spill light* from an open window, or a suburban garage, or a faded letter dyes the winter leaves of the old roses green.

In the darkest of skies, theoretical or not, Mother, here are the words for light I can give you: *effulgence,* meaning a *shining forth.* Or *incandescence: the emission of visible light by a body.* Or, finally, *luminescence*—all that gold light we can see, like a husband's or a father's or now a mother's, which does not need the body's heat to warm us.

THE CALVES OF WINTER

ISABELLE, OUR DECEPTIVELY POOFED and perfumed poodle—
known to choke down a half-frozen rabbit whole despite the
tug of war over the bloody, mountain lion-cached carcass with
her mitten-wearing owner (me)—sniffed the calf out first, a
black comma typeset into the early February snow.

Too soon.

At 9600 feet, a polar inversion had just threatened the
kitchen sink pipes and the ever-present, "oh my god," arctic
wind tunneled the snow into crevice and cliff. The hovering
mother Angus, anxious and postpartum, head-butted at
Isabelle romping too close to her tongue-wet newborn.

For years now, Dave's Angus cows drift from spring to
early winter across the high meadows, a dark tide I follow in
summer, ebbing and flowing around the circumferences of
these forty acre plots where berms the vanished ranchers once
dug into the draws pool into holding ponds, collect snowmelt
and the long white bones of elk and cow I stroke my fingers
along, harps of rib I pluck as if silence were song.

"Cows?" Leonard repeats, when I tell him what I am
writing. "That's a thrill," and then disappears to tend his fish
tank.

But I am my mother's daughter. I grew up in the Midwest
with cows. I saw them birthed; saw them stillborn, their
bloody sacs flagging in the air; saw them shot in the head
with pistols, then heaved in chains to the top of barn doors
and skinned, the ground black with their blood. I felt them
divide as a river around me, pinned behind a tree in their torn
unstoppable wake. I found calves in the woods, fed them with
a bucket and nipple until they could suck my whole hand into

their loamy mouths. I have parted them on horseback, the underbrush beneath the river cottonwoods shaking with the unseen until a whole herd of longhorns catapulted into the clearing, my horse rearing, circling in their diffraction.

I surprise myself sometimes with how much I have forgotten of Ohio, the home my mother mourns so daily, even though its grace notes hover beneath everything I write and love: the long rolling highways that vanish around the bends of trees, the irregular cornfields and the soybean fields bleached by such heat and humidity it is as if light from a distance lifted. Or the constant cicada drill, sound of insects I seldom hear at 9600 feet except in late summer when the winged grasshoppers I remember from childhood rasp past— ugly sound but beautiful wings the folded legs hide. Or the tall wild flowers, weeds I thought them when I was a girl, Queen Anne's Lace and their small folds of blue flowers, and chicory like rumpled silk dissolving between my fingers into blue stain. But I do remember the steaming breath of cows waiting in the barnyard beneath the loft window for the hay my mother—*every god-forsaken winter,* she likes to grumble—tossed out for them, gold explosion beneath the gray midwestern sky.

"Like home," Mother said, homesick as Ruth in the *alien corn* of the poet Keats, when she first saw the Angus cows grazing our leased land.

Like Buddhas, I thought them.

Tathāgata: "thus come, thus gone."

I drag Isabelle from the wobbling calf and half-run the hill to wave my cell phone at the capricious electromagnetic waves of the nearest cell phone tower and call Dave. He knows the cow I'm talking about and tells me that several of his heifers have birthed calves in the fields this year.

"A little too soon," he adds.

South of the cabin, I tell him, and he promises to drive over later. I fret and cut an empty water container in half with the kitchen scissors, fill it with water and slog downhill, carrying a bag of dinner salad for the mother, who stares at me blankly—"Dinner salad?" Dave chuckles later—and then charges at Isabelle zeroed in on her calf again until I throw myself at this panting, cockatiel-killing frou frou—another story—and catch a single finger under her pink deco collar.

In the mid 1880s, Colorado was a part of the "Great Die-Off." In the Great Plains, an extreme winter, overgrazed land and an unexpected surge of cattle from the Indian Territory reportedly ignited the death of 90% of the cattle allowed to free range untended, even over winter. Piles of cow carcasses marked the territory while the few that remained hobbled snow-blighted and emaciated, half-corpse among the corpses. Contemporary researchers do cast doubt on this death toll claim. They cite disparate "eye-witness" testimonies and greedy territorial cattlemen who may have used the perceived phenomena as a way to "clean up" their accounting and keep new cattlemen at bay. Yet, the Great Die-Off drastically changed the free-wheeling cowboy way of cattle-driving, glorified by Hollywood B list movies, into more practical cattle-management practices, soon sustaining the grasslands and the cattle with fencing and winter-haying, a practice evidenced by the spools of old barbed wire I stumble over, half-buried in the grass with the bones of lost cows.

Morning, I take Isabelle and the good mutt Joey up the lane, away from the calf and its anxious mother. But to no avail. What I perceived as two black stumps half-buried in the snow are actually calves.

Dead, I think. Frozen.

Isabelle leaps over the snow drifts before I can stop her and strong-arms the motionless calves I name too soon "carcasses" with her "dainty" poodle tongue until one flinches.

Curses. Headlock. I wrestle Isabelle down the lane to call Dave again, Joey stoically trotting alongside this carnivorous poodle, coiffed *"Caniche"—duck dog*.

Teller County has a "local right-to-farm-and-ranch" policy. According to Teller County, some of the consequences of living in rural Colorado, such as the evening cacophony of mother and calf reunions after a day of mother-grazing afar and those cow pies the size of dinner platters that occasionally land on our porch steps from apparently enormous, fiber-eating bulls, cannot be considered nuisances by the same "city folk" who venture out into the rural and mountains land. Colorado as a "fence out" state means cattle owners are not responsible for keeping their cattle fenced in. We, the flat-landers, must fence the cattle out. Cattle breeders from the plains can truck their cattle to these mountain plains, the cattle tending to themselves until these owners return at the end of summer to trailer them to the slaughterhouses. But for Dave and Tandy, their free-range, grass-fed, hormone-free beef business is a full-time operation, a constant sleuthing out of cattle from horseback and four wheelers as they shift their cows across 2000 acres of leased private and Bureau of Land Management grassland, our forty acres included.

"The neighbor's bull," Dave tells me over the cell phone, when I ask what happened, frantic at the specter of apparently abandoned baby calves dotting everywhere this winter wasteland. Neither the costly, genetically-suited dynamo that Dave and Tandy sought out for their beloved, cookie-loving heifers nor the barbed wire, "Devil's Rope," the frontiersmen called it, were a match for the machismo of the bull next door, which tore down the fence, battered the young Sir Lancelot senseless beneath a tree and then impregnated some twenty fair Guineveres.

While researching the love life of cows, I run across a *New York Times*' expose on the decades-long cruelty to farm animals by the U.S. Meat Animal Research Center in Nebraska. Founded 50 years ago by Congress to help livestock producers improve the profits of cattlemen on the global market, the research center was designed to "to re-engineer the farm animal to fit the needs of the 21st-century meat industry." Yet, starvation tactics and grotesque breeding experiments have often resulted in fetal deformities and excruciating death for the farm animals. The 60's Federal Animal Welfare Act ignited campaigns for the humane treatment of animals and made grass-roots industries like Dave and Tandy's a fiscal possibility. But a loophole in the Act exempts "farm animals used in research to benefit agriculture" from humane treatment and has allowed the research center to continue practices I can barely read. For example, it tested cattle with growth hormones already pulled from the market by the manufacturer itself because of "hooves that slough off" after treatment and it denied experimentation with more "effective pain medicine" for simple surgical procedures because, as the center self-disclosed, it couldn't "assess the pain felt by animals," an inability apparently not shared by the mother cows that wander these acres.

Dave trucks over the horizon just as I, in all despair, stumble onto the scene of what I am sure will be poodle mayhem and calf death. Two summers ago, Leonard and I headed down the valley with the dogs when we heard a sound we'd never heard before—like some exotic bird in drift migration calling across continents. Leonard hobbled past me, yelling at me to come down, that the "damn poodle" had seized a fawn from beneath a stump—Joey simply observing. "I can't run," he yells, his knee bad before the future surgery that would fix it, somehow all this symbolizing our marriage: what we'd come to after thirty years, me half-running, half-limping past my gruff and kind husband to help him save the fawn, afraid of my bad hip, every ounce of breath I could take in my lungs summoned to bellow obscenities at the poodle, and the fawn, so helpless, how so utterly it gave up when Isabelle finally dropped it, flattening itself on the ground, chin thrust forward, back legs sprawled, its fur where Isabelle had put her mouth on it damp and sticky. When I touched it, when I felt its small frail bones beneath the pliant back, the fawn sprang up, squealed once more like a winged thing and disappeared into the woods, *Tathāgata*, come and gone.

The caustic attitude of the U.S. Meat Animal Research Center is nothing new. In 2013, Amy Meyer became the first person charged with violating Ag-Gag laws when she videotaped the "killing floor" of Dale T. Smith and Sons Meat Packing Company in Draper, Utah, even though it was reported that she was clearly standing on public land and not trespassing as accused. Ag-Gag laws were the outgrowth of the "Animal and Ecological Terrorism Act," drafted in the early 2000's by the American Legislative Exchange Council, a forum of state legislators and private citizens. The idea was to draft model legislation for states to modify for their own purposes, such as the Ag-Gag laws.

Ag-Gag laws have been "anti-whistleblower," created to keep citizen activists from recording activities like the floor-slamming "euthanasia" of baby piglets at West Coast Farms in January 2014, Tyson Foods only terminating its contract with West Coast Farms after NBC aired the undercover video footage, *Mercy for Animals*. According to the American Society for the Prevention of Cruelty to Animals, while Ag-Gag bills failed in twenty-four states, at least five have passed their own version of the Ag-Gag bill. Colorado's own version, a "quick-reporting" bill, required whistleblowers to report cruelty in 48 hours, preventing any meaningful investigation and evidence collection. It died out in the Judiciary Committee. But the Ag-Gag bill, despite protestations of humaneness by all, has been introduced across the country.

Two mother cows lumber over the rise, anxious for their calves dead still in the grass. Dave and I sit on the back of his truck, wiggling nutrient-rich cow "cookies" at the mothers, who graciously accept them.

"The real problem," Dave says, "is figuring out which baby belongs to which mama." It turns out that leaving baby calves scattered around a field is common herd practice, allowing the mothers to graze and build up their milk reserves.

We watch the mother cows nose their calves in the grass, the "correct" baby springing up to nuzzle at its mother's udder before heading back to the distant herd, firmly ensconced in its mother's care. Before long the neighbors show up, riding up on horseback or four-wheeler, properly trained ranch dogs trotting at their sides, the hysterical Isabelle condemned to a crate.

We circle the herd, inch the placid mothers and their bobbling babies up the lane to Phantom Canyon and the rickety community cattle corral where Dave and the ranchers ear tag the calves before he trailers them all toward barn and sweet hay.

Above us rise the snow-stippled flanks of Nipple Mountain. Soon spring. Soon warmth: bluebirds dipping over the last slippers of snow and the cattle my mother and I love returned, lowing their calves into the evening grass.

Yes, one day, *Tathāgata*, come then gone, but gently.

CODA

AT THE CABIN this weekend, above this canyon of phantoms that you told me you will never visit again—"I feel safe here," you say now of the assisted living center you other days hate—I rearrange the three framed birds you embroidered in honor of your mother, who taught you this thousand-year art of needle and thread, what you taught me so long ago that I have forgotten it.

I didn't imagine this. I thought blindness meant impermeable darkness, not this obscuring of the visible and the invisible, the obscuring of you, woman who bore me, cared for me, loved me as much as she could, who shared with me her love of solitary birds and murmuring trees. I think, in the beginning, I imagined myself some winged goddess carrying a silent and stoic mother across a long sky stitched with rushes, stitched with some field of knotted gold, some leaf dark red from a childhood we both keep mourning.

But I am nothing of that.

You are nothing of that.

I keep asking you, *what do you see?* you who have lamented over your inevitable blindness for twenty years but could see until now a grain of dirt on my floor, a smear on my kitchen cabinets.

Once, I wrote a child's poem: "My Mother Needlepoints." I had forgotten how many years, days, hours, moments I watched you stitch in companionship with my father as he watched TV after his long doctor's day.

In and out, I wrote, *her silver needle flashes, in and out.*

I take you down to the river. Not that river of myth where one day we will perhaps forget everything, but the suburban one where you walk faster than me, where I have to grab your elbows so you don't fall over, where you hover over a log you want to sit on, as stilled in the air, until I pull you down, as the hummingbirds at my feeder, as the tiny birds you stitched and I hold in these wooden picture frames. We sit and you tell me, as you always do, that you are not happy with life, as if I didn't know, as if when I call you on the phone and ask how you are, I don't hear the tiny frayed thread of you.

Go back to Ohio, I say. *Let's change where you live,* I say.

No, you say.

"Oh, no," the nurses at the assisted living center tell me when I say how sad you are. "She tells us she is happy. She is good."

In and out, her silver needle flashes, her yarn whispering of goldenrod and eggshell.

Someone who read this asked me if I were not one of the frail children, too, like my father became, like you, and I thought of your hands, how Leonard always says he sees them: the way you bring your palms together now above your lap, not in stitch or prayer, how you rub your thumbs together, the joints of your fingers that I have watched my whole life sew and embroider, cross stitch and knit, misshapen now, impossibly fluted, your veins all blue yarn and bruise. And how I find myself rubbing my thumbs together, too.

"*My skin too thin,*" you always say of the dark that flowers out of you.

You always said you would die by seventy-two, when your mother died, but I think now that you and your sisters inherited the genes of your father, the man who gave you and me his black hair, mine more silver than yours now, the mystery man I only know as a boy from a 1918 photo of your mother's 16th birthday, not yet the young man of family fame I heard

132

about for jumping rail road cars, *young hobo*, you called him, wanderer until he married my grandmother, your mother, at twenty-six.

The boy in the white shirt is my dad, you wrote in your caption for the family genealogy.

"I think at my age," you say while we wait, *"I should be going soon,"* you too tired to walk down the banks of this river you already keep forgetting. I can think only to joke with you: something inane about your having no oxygen tank, no walker, still traces of your father's black hair, so *"don't hold your breath."* We both laugh and walk.

Only your head a little troubled, I don't tell you. *Only your eyes, those little shades.*

Of cornflower, I wrote in my children's poem, *and bedtime plum.*

Am I one of the frail children? I want to say that I am the daughter of a private woman, a woman of strength and great creativity, though you hid this so carefully: *Why don't you enter your tapestries into the assisted living show?* I ask you. *You know I don't do things like that*, you say, you, this woman of childhood attics, of *black moods*, as your own mother called them, of a genetic tendency toward days of menstrual bleeding out that you shared with great grandmothers and cousins I've only heard of, *one who died*, you always like to tell me between your weeping and your forgetting, *hemorrhaged out*, what I thought of the day in the coffeeshop bathroom when my own blood flooded and I stood there crying, trying to clean myself, *frail child*, the door I had forgotten to lock swinging open.

Beneath her hands, warm as milk, I wrote, *her silver needle flashes.*

Am I one of the frail children? I know the tug of yarn and embroidery thread, the smooth threshing of cross stitches across whole counted worlds we created tiniest stitch by stitch, silk of a worm we could knot and weave into a square of linen, into a life, our lives, needles both of us can hardly see passing in now and out.

Your youngest sister dies and you weep like a child. I press my palm against your leg or shoulder, burn of my eyes betraying me. The life you had, what you send me to my aunt's, to your youngest sister's, funeral to tell: your mother giving birth in the room next to you and your middle sister, not a sound, you say, until the newborn mewed like a lamb, you making the sound out loud for me, you and your sister never knowing your mother carried this tiny girl until then.

We adored her, you keep saying, this sister four days dead you keep weeping over.

And I watch birds fly

I did not know you had such sadness. I did not know there was this tenderness within you, this frailty, petal soft my father must have known and loved, lying with you in those dark canyons of your own making, whispering what, I wonder, while my brother and sister and I slept rooms apart.

If I were only there, I could do something, you keep crying, my mother-blind, my mother-seer of this unraveling world, phantom of this canyon you've given me, mother who will keep pushing me away, some deep room, some old attic your mother once swept clean for you, closed to me.

And how the garden roses, I wrote, *in winter bloom.*

Sadness carried me today—sadness of you, sadness for a red tree a student wept over when she read her poem out loud to my class that no one else would ever weep over. I remember, because I was thinking of you that day, how I changed the word "love" to "despair" on the whiteboard in front of that class, which barely knew poetry, and asked them to think again about the images they had given me to write down: *What does your black car driving fast mean now? Or your red tree? Or this trailing list of herbs called out by one of you, sick with a toddler's cough: nettles and lavender, goldenrod?*

What of these images, perhaps I should ask of myself, *written here?*

ACKNOWLEDGMENTS

Of everyone, I want to thank my mother first for giving me and my family what we missed all those years before she moved here—her delightful companionship, no matter what the day, and genuine friendship. I thank her, too, for the gift and love of writing that I realize so clearly now she gave me. Leonard, constant companion for more than thirty-nine years, of course, is next, and if I could, as he has requested, I would put his name in fifty-point font. No matter what I do, he is always there beside me: love, peer, first reader and, for this project, copyeditor and genesis for the idea of the Coda to this book. And our daughters, Kitty and Mira, who ever since our first glimpse of our "fric and frac" on that early blurred sonogram have made our world more beautiful every day. And to John, our newest family member.

I also want to thank the editors who published five of the original essays in this book: *Arts & Letters*, *River Teeth*, *The Fourth Genre*, *Juxtaprose*, and *Inverted Syntax*. Each publication made me realize that this book could be a possibility. And thank you to the Bread Loaf Orion Environmental Writers' Conference, which awarded me a small scholarship based on two of the essays in this collection: *Slow Arrow* and *The Calves of Winter*; and to *Winning Writers*, which republished *Breviaries of the Ghost* as an honorable mention for its *Tom*

Howard/John H. Reid Fiction & Essay Contest. Thank you, too, *Inverted Syntax* editors for the Pushcart Prize nomination of *Slow Arrow*. And a special thank you to Tom Larson for not only his helpful comments on the manuscript, but for his invitation to join him, Janice Gary, Shann Ray, and Beverly Donofrio for an AWP panel on "Writing the Spiritual Memoir." *On Intla: Snow that has Drifted Indoors,* as it appears now, is a direct result of that panel.

I am grateful to the wonderful writers and friends who have served as inspiration, sounding boards, and guides over the years to so much of this book. I especially treasure the years I spent with the creative nonfiction and poetry faculty at Ashland University's original MFA program—fabulous generous writers all. Special thanks to Steve Haven and Joe Mackall who created an incredible, supportive writing oasis in poetry and creative nonfiction alike for students and faculty. And special thanks to Robert Root, Steve Harvey, Tom Larson, Jill Christman, and Sonya Huber who, with so much warmth, encouraged me in my first endeavors in creative nonfiction. Many thanks to Annie Dawid, long time friend and writing confidante, who first put me on the path to this book by encouraging me to apply to a since defunct journalism site, *Beacon,* where the germ of these essays began. Thanks to my former colleagues and writing support group at Arapahoe Community College, Monica Fuglei, Andrea Mason, Juliet Hubbell, and Lindsay Lewan, who encouraged me through the earlier drafts of this book.

Thank you to Greg Hobbs for his beautiful moon photo that begins the essay, "Skyglow" and to Liz Netzel for her spacious sky and clouds photo that begins "Migration Corridors."

Much thanks and gratitude to Ruth Thompson, editor, and Don Mitchell, book designer, at Saddle Road Press, who surprised and awed me with their immediate embrace of this book. I could not have found more responsive, responsible, enthusiastic, and just darn friendly editors to share this journey with.

And, finally, thanks to my 9600 ft neighbors for their wonderful stories, friendship, and shared love for this beautiful place we all call home.

"Breviaries of the Ghost, "*Arts & Letters*, republished nonfiction, honorable mention: Tom Howard/John H. Reid Fiction & Essay Contest 2016

"On Intla: Snow that has Drifted Indoors," *River Teeth Journal*

"Skyglow," *The Fourth Genre*

"Slow Arrow," *Inverted Syntax*, nominated for Pushcart Prize

"Unearthing the Frail Children," *Juxtaprose*

"Gravitational Waves," finalist 2019 *Fourth Genre* Steinberg Essay Contest

ABOUT THE AUTHOR

Kathryn Winograd is the author of *Phantom Canyon: Essays of Reclamation*, a finalist for the Foreword Reviews' 2014 #INDIEFAB Book of the Year Nonfiction (Essays) Award, and *Air Into Breath*, which won the Colorado Book Award in Poetry.

Her essays have been noted in *Best American Essays*, and published in many journals and anthologies.

Her poetry has received three Pushcart Prize nominations and a Special Mention in Pushcart Prize XXXVIII.

She has been the recipient of a Colorado Artist Fellowship in Poetry, a Rocky Mountain Women's Institute Associateship, and a co-winner of a Colorado Endowment for The Humanities Grant.

CASSANDRA VACHER

She received her Ph.D. in Literature and Creative Writing from the University of Denver, and a M.F.A. in poetry from the University of Iowa.

She divides her time between Littleton and a cabin off Phantom Canyon road with her husband, a mutt named Joey, and a frou frou poodle turned master hunter, Isabelle.

CPSIA information can be obtained
at www.ICGtesting.com
Printed in the USA
FFHW021301210120
57943215-63131FF